Analysis and Metaphysics

Analysis and Metaphysics

AN INTRODUCTION TO PHILOSOPHY

P. F. Strawson

OXFORD UNIVERSITY PRESS

1992

Oxford University Press, Walton Street, Oxford OX2 6DP
Oxford New York Toronto
Delhi Bombay Calcutta Madras Karachi
Petaling Jaya Singapore Hong Kong Tokyo
Nairobi Dar es Salaam Cape Town
Melbourne Auckland
and associated companies in
Berlin Ibadan

Oxford is a trade mark of Oxford University Press

Published in the United States
by Oxford University Press, New York

British Library Cataloguing in Publication Data
Data available

Library of Congress Cataloging in Publication Data
Strawson, P. F.
Analysis and metaphysics: an introduction to philosophy / P.F.
Strawson.
p. cm.
1. Philosophy. I. Title.
B29.S8216 1992   100—dc20   91–36879
ISBN 0–19–875117–6
ISBN 0–19–875118–4 (pbk.)

Typeset by Hope Services (Abingdon) Ltd.
Printed in Great Britain by
Biddles Ltd., Guildford & King's Lynn

To
Ann Strawson

Preface

I DESCRIBE this book as an introduction to philosophy. It is introductory in two ways. First, it presupposes, on the part of its readers, no prior acquaintance with the subject. It should be capable of being understood without any such acquaintance. Second, it begins, not with the discussion of particular problems, but with an account of the general nature of philosophy as, in common with many other philosophers of our period, I conceive of and try to practise it. (There are, of course, other legitimate conceptions.)

This general account gradually merges into an attempt to show, in outline, how some of the major issues which arise in the connected fields of metaphysics, epistemology, and the philosophy of language can, and should, be resolved. Then, finally, two particular philosophical questions are chosen to be treated, in the concluding chapters, in greater illustrative detail. So the progression is from the global to the local, from the general to the specific, from the outline to the detail.

The book, then, may fairly be described as introductory. But, though introductory, it is not elementary. There is no such thing as elementary philosophy. There is no shallow end to the philosophical pool.

Something must now be said about the work's genesis. For almost every year from 1968 until my retirement in 1987 I gave, in Oxford, a series of sixteen introductory lectures in philosophy under the present title. The first seven chapters of this book preserve, virtually unchanged, the content of the first ten or eleven of the 1968 lectures, to which I made few alterations in succeeding years. The matter of Chapter 8 was incorporated later in the lectures at a time when Tarski-inspired truth-theoretical theories of meaning for natural language were becoming popular. The choice of particular philosophical issues, to be treated in greater detail in the concluding lectures, varied over the years with my current preoccupations, and included, at one time, the themes of the last two chapters of this book.

Finally, a word about the use that has been made of all this material up to the present. The last two chapters were published, respectively, in *Essays on Davidson: Actions and Events*, ed. Vermazen and Hintikka (Oxford, 1985) and *Spinoza: His Thought and Work* (Jerusalem, 1983). I am grateful to the editors and publishers of these volumes for permission to reproduce them here. The entire work, with a few omissions, notably that of Chapter 8, I translated into French and delivered as lectures in the Collège de France in the spring of 1985. (These lectures, under the title *Analyse et métaphysique*, were published later in that year in Paris by J. Vrin.) I delivered substantially the same lectures with some omissions as the Immanuel Kant lectures in Munich in the summer of 1985; in the Catholic University of America in Washington in September 1987; and as my contribution to the Sino-British Summer School in philosophy in Beijing in the summer of 1988. So the lectures as a whole have been extensively aired, but not previously published in English.

I dedicate the book to my wife, whose company and support, both on all these occasions and throughout my working life, have been of immeasurable help and value to me.

P. F. S.

Oxford
May 1991

Contents

❖ 1 ❖

Analytical Philosophy
Two Analogies

As remarked in the Preface, my first task—that of trying to explain the general conception of philosophy to which I am committed—will lead into a sketch of the main divisions of the subject, of some of the main issues that arise within it, and of their interconnections; and this will be followed, in conclusion, with a more detailed illustrative treatment of two specific issues.

Of course, that great name, 'philosophy', has not always, at all times, meant just one and the same thing. Neither does it now, for everyone, have precisely the same significance. The point can be illustrated in many ways. It can even, perhaps surprisingly, be illustrated from English poetry. Not that the word occurs there very frequently; but it does occur sometimes. Thus, a character in Milton's masque *Comus*, says: 'How charming is divine philosophy.' John Keats, on the other hand, in his poem *Lamia*, seems to say almost the exact opposite: 'Do not all charms fly at the mere touch of cold philosophy?'

The opposition is only apparent. It is clear enough from the context that they are really talking about different things under the same name. Keats was talking about what until comparatively recently was still called 'natural philosophy' and is now called 'natural science' or simply 'science'. His point, or part of it, was that science was inimical to fantasy and myth and the exercise of the poetic imagination. ('Philosophy will clip an angel's wings', etc.). He had, perhaps, a more philosophical point (in another sense) to make when he added that philosophy, i.e. science, will 'unweave a rainbow'; and we will come back to that.

Milton had something quite different in mind from natural science. His character's remark follows upon, and refers to, a long and splendid declamation in favour of chastity—a declamation which can still be found charming, even if, in these days, a little quaint. And *his* point, I suppose, is that eloquent reasoned reflection upon the moral nature of man can soothe and fortify and elevate the spirit. Now, the use of the word 'philosophy' for something akin to this kind of meditation is not outdated in the way that its use to stand for what we now call 'science' is outdated. On the contrary. There is a species of philosophy which flourishes still, and will no doubt continue to flourish as long as men continue to meditate on their moral nature and situation. I refer to that kind of more or less systematic reflection on the human situation which one finds in the work of, say, Heidegger, Sartre, and Nietzsche, and which, indeed, largely dominated their work—a kind of reflection which can sometimes lead to a new perspective on human life and experience.

The analytical philosopher, on the other hand—at least as I conceive him—promises no such new and revealing vision. His aim is something quite different.

What is it, then, his aim? What is he concerned with? Well, with ideas or concepts, surely. So his self-awarded title of 'analytical philosopher' suggests 'conceptual analysis' as the favoured description of his favoured activity. And perhaps that will serve well enough as a name. Taken seriously as a description, it may be less satisfactory. An analysis, I suppose, may be thought of as a kind of breaking down or decomposing of something. So we have the picture of a kind of intellectual taking to pieces of ideas or concepts; the discovering of what elements a concept or idea is composed and how they are related. Is this the right picture or the wrong one—or is it partly right and partly wrong? That is a question which calls for a considered response—a response I shall defer till later.

We are offered other pictures from time to time, some of them overtly analogies or metaphors. Professor Ryle, for example, used to speak of conceptual geography or conceptual mapping or charting. This picture has merits. A map or chart gives us a representation of an area, a representation which is in some measure abstract and such as we do not ordinarily get through normal perceptual encounters. Maps can vary in scale, show more or less detail, reflect different particular interests. They can help us to get about. With an accurate chart we are less likely to suffer shipwreck; and intellectual or conceptual shipwreck is surely a possibility.

All the same, the picture remains uncomfortably metaphorical. If we discard the metaphorical elements, we are left simply with the notion of an abstract representation of certain relations between certain concepts made for a certain purpose. But what concepts, what relations, what purpose? All this is, so far, unspecified.

Another, quite different image, which has been familiar for some time, yet may still seem surprising, is that of the analytical philosopher as a kind of therapist, who undertakes to cure certain characteristic kinds of intellectual disorder. He offers no doctrine, no theory; rather, he brings to bear a technique. When we try to think at a philosophical level, we are apt, according to this view, to fall into certain obsessive muddles or confusions; to see ourselves as led by reason to conclusions which we can neither accept nor escape from; to ask questions which seem to have no answers or only absurd answers; to become unable to see how what we know very well to be the case can possibly be the case; and so on. The role of the analytical philosopher is then to straighten us out or to help us to straighten ourselves out; to free us from the obsessive confusions, the false models which dominate our thinking, and to enable us to see clearly what is in front of us. Thus Wittgenstein says: 'The philosopher's treatment of a question is like the treatment of an illness.'[1] We are to go to him, it seems, somewhat as a neurotic goes to an analyst.

Now this conception, this picture of the philosopher as therapist, may seem very implausible, perhaps even shocking; at least exaggerated and one-sided. And I think it is, in fact, exaggerated and one-sided. But it is certainly worth considering further; for it too has merit. It prompts questions to which its adherents have given answers. The questions are: how do these characteristic disorders arise? What forms do they take? And how are they cured or

---

[1] Wittgenstein, *Philosophical Investigations*, § 255.

corrected? In general: how do we get into the typical philosophical impasse? And how do we get out?

The answer that is offered is this: that these disorders never arise when our concepts, our ideas, are actually at work; but only when they are idle. Of course we may get into other sorts of muddles, encounter other sorts of problems, when we are using the words which express our ideas to do the work which is properly theirs; but we never get into philosophical muddles or encounter philosophical problems. We get into these muddles, encounter these problems, only when we allow the concepts or the words to become detached from their actual use, from the practical or theoretical concerns which give them their significance; when we allow them to float or race idly through our minds. When this happens, all sorts of superficial grammatical parallels, or deep-buried figures or metaphors, or inappropriate models or pictures, may take charge of our thinking and lead us into paradox or absurdity or myth or hopeless confusion. These distorting influences, though always latent, are neutralized so long as our words or concepts are actually being exploited in the various theoretical or practical spheres which are their true field of operation. But when the words, the concepts, are not at work, but loose in the mind and on the tongue, then we (and they) are at the mercy of these same distorting influences.

This, then, is the diagnosis; and given the diagnosis, the nature of the cure is clear. The wildly racing, but idle, intellectual engine must be engaged. The hold of the obsessive, illusory models must be broken by our being forcefully and effectively reminded of the reality, that is of the actual employment of the words and concepts concerned. This is the point of Wittgenstein's slogan: 'Don't look for the meaning, look for the use.' This is why he says: 'The work of the philosopher consists in assembling reminders for a particular purpose';[2] and also: 'What *we* do is to bring words back from their metaphysical to their everyday usage.'[3]

In the eyes of many of those who are customarily called analytical philosophers, this view of what the nature of their activity is, or ought to be, has seemed totally repugnant and frivolous—a total

[2] Wittgenstein, *Philosophical Investigations*, § 127.
[3] Ibid. § 116.

abdication, as it were, of philosophical responsibility. So it seemed, for example, to Lord Russell, and so it seems to Sir Karl Popper. Their comments on the later work of Wittgenstein have a peculiar bitterness. But extreme positions are rarely right. So there is a general presumption that an extreme position on this question is wrong; that it would equally be a mistake to embrace the therapeutic position to the exclusion of everything else or to repudiate it utterly.

Let us leave this question, and this analogy of therapy, on one side for a while, and consider, instead, another analogy. Like all analogies, it has its dangers. But since it seems to me more promising than the others, I shall take the risks and develop the analogy at some length.

When the first Spanish or, strictly, Castilian grammar was presented to Queen Isabella of Castile, her response was to ask what use it was. The reply made on behalf of the grammarian was of a world-historical character, referring to language as an instrument of empire—and that need no longer concern us. What does concern us is the point of her question. For of course the grammar was in a certain sense of no use at all to fluent speakers of Castilian. In a sense they knew it all already. They spoke grammatically correct Castilian because grammatically correct Castilian simply *was* what they spoke. The grammar did not set the standard of correctness for the sentences they spoke; on the contrary, it was the sentences they spoke that set the standard of correctness for the grammar. However, though in a sense they knew the grammar of their language, there was another sense in which they did not know it.

If Isabella had been asked to state, in a maximally systematic way, a system of rules or principles in the light of which one could decide, with respect to any sequence of Castilian words, whether or not it constituted a grammatically complete and correct sentence, she would have been quite at a loss. Her practice and that of her courtiers, in constructing Castilian sentences, showed that she and they in a sense observed such a set or system of rules or principles. Her and their practice was in a sense governed by such rules or principles. But from the fact that she and they effortlessly observed the rules it by no means follows that they could, effortlessly or with an effort, state the rules, say what they were.

We can draw the general moral that being able to do something—in this case speak grammatically—is very different from being able to say how it's done; and that it by no means implies the latter. Mastery of a practice does not involve an explicit mastery (though it may sometimes be allowed to involve an implicit mastery) of the theory of that practice. Grammars were implicitly mastered long before grammars were ever explicitly written; and implicit grammars are necessary to speech and therefore necessary to any but the most rudimentary thinking. But of course rational human beings, capable of developed thinking, must have an implicit mastery of more than grammars; or, rather, their implicit mastery of their grammars is intertwined with an implicit mastery of all the concepts, all the general ideas which find expression in their speech, which they operate with in their thought. In our transactions with each other and the world we operate with an enormously rich, complicated, and refined conceptual equipment; but we are not, and indeed could not be, taught the mastery of the items of this formidable equipment by being taught the *theory* of their employment.

Thus, for example, we know, in a sense, what knowing is perfectly well long before we hear (if we ever do hear) of the Theory of Knowledge. We know, in one sense, what it is to speak the truth without perhaps suspecting that there are such things as Theories of Truth. We learn to handle the words 'the same', 'real', 'exists', and to handle them correctly, without being aware of the philosophical problems of Identity, Reality, and Existence. In the same way, we learn to operate with a vast and heterogeneous range of notions: ethical notions: good, bad, right, wrong, punishment; temporal and spatial concepts; the ideas of causality and explanation; ideas of emotions: sadness, anger, fear, joy; of mental operations of various kinds: thinking, believing, wondering, remembering, expecting, imagining; of perception and sense experience: seeing, hearing, touching, having sensations; whole ranges of classificatory concepts for types of people, animals, plants, natural objects, processes, or events, human artefacts, institutions, and roles; and the properties, qualities, doings, and undergoings of all these. Of course we learn the words which express these concepts in a variety of ways; but we learn them largely without benefit of anything which could properly be called general theoretical instruction. We are not introduced to them by being told their place in a general theory of concepts. Such instruction as we do receive is severely practical and largely by example. We learn largely by copying and by occasional correction; as children learn to speak grammatically before they hear of grammars.

To press on, then, with the analogy. Just as we may have a working mastery of the grammar of our native language, so we have a working mastery of this conceptual equipment. We know how to handle it, how to use it in thought and speech. But just as the practical mastery of the grammar in no way entails the ability to state systematically what the rules are which we effortlessly observe, so the practical mastery of our conceptual equipment in no way entails the possession of a clear, explicit understanding of the principles which govern our handling of it, of the theory of our practice. So— to conclude the analogy—just as the grammarian, and especially the model modern grammarian, labours to produce a systematic account of the structure of rules which we effortlessly observe in speaking grammatically, so the philosopher labours to produce a systematic account of the general *conceptual structure* of which our daily practice shows us to have a tacit and unconscious mastery.

In one sense—to repeat an example—we understand the concept of knowing, we know what knowing is or what the word 'know' means; for we know how to use the word correctly. In one sense we understand the concept of personal identity, we know what sameness of person is, we know what the words 'same person' mean; for we know in practice how to apply the concept; and if, sometimes, we have difficulty in deciding questions of identity, these are practical, law-court difficulties, not conceptual difficulties. But in another sense, perhaps, we don't understand the concepts, don't know what personal identity is, can't say what the word 'know' means. We have mastered a practice, but can't state the theory of our practice. We know the rules because we observe them and yet we don't know them because we can't say what they are. In contrast with the ease and accuracy of our use are the stuttering and blundering which characterize our first attempts to describe and explain our use.

This account, this analogy of grammar, like its predecessors, gives rise to doubts, queries, questions. By examining them, we may get a better idea of its merits and its limitations and so work our way towards something more satisfactory, more comprehensive, and less figurative.

First, an objection. It might be said that it is quite untrue that we do not and cannot quite ordinarily say what our concepts are, what our words mean. We often give and receive explicit instruction of just this kind—which does not make, of those who give or receive such instruction, either philosophers or philosophers' pupils. Part of the answer to this objection is to ask: whoever told you what the word 'same' means or the word 'know' or the word 'if' or the word 'meaning' or the phrase 'the reason why' or 'there is'—all in your own native language? And to whom did you ever explain what these expressions in his native language mean? So here is one set of key concepts—*identity, knowledge, meaning, explanation, existence*—which we learn to handle successfully, but to which we were never introduced by explicit instruction. The rest of the answer is this: such explicit instruction in meanings as we do receive and give in the ordinary way is strictly practical in intent and effect. Its aim is to get us to be able to understand, and to use, expressions in practice. It presupposes the antecedent mastery of an existing conceptual structure and uses any techniques to hand for modifying and enriching it; whereas the principles, the structure, the explanations which the analytical philosopher is in search of are not to be reached by any of these strictly practical techniques; for they are precisely the principles, the structure, an implicit grasp of which is presupposed by the use of these techniques.

So much for that objection. But now, second, the following query might be raised: what are the relations between this account of the philosophical task, which uses the analogy of grammar, and the Wittgensteinian account which uses the analogy of therapy? Clearly they have a considerable amount in common. They both place great weight on the actual use of concepts in the spheres which are properly theirs—be they the ordinary concerns of daily life or the professional concerns of engineers, physiologists, historians, accountants, or mathematicians. They both suggest that, somehow, the saving truth lies there, in the actual employment of concepts. Nevertheless, it is evident that the spirit and the aims of the two analogies are significantly different. In the grammatical analogy there is the suggestion of a system; of a general underlying structure to be laid bare; even of explanation. There is the suggestion that we might come to add to our practical mastery something like a theoretical understanding of what we are doing when we exercise that mastery. The therapeutic analogy, on the other hand, seems to be conceived in a more negative spirit. We are not to construct a system, but to 'assemble reminders' for a particular purpose; and this purpose is that of liberating ourselves from the confusions and perplexities we get into when our concepts are idling in the mind; when we suppose ourselves to be reflecting very seriously and very deeply, but when in fact our ideas, free from the discipline of their actual use, are free also to make fools of us, to mislead us by all kinds of analogies and pictures—analogies and pictures which are, in a sense, already in the language, but normally harmlessly there, because neutralized by the words being at work, the work which gives them all the significance they have. So, according to this conception, the philosopher explains nothing except, perhaps, the source of our confusions, how they arise. Otherwise, we are simply to be reminded, by reference to cases, actual or imagined, of what we knew all along, that is, of how the words are actually and ordinarily used. Then the philosophical problem is solved in the only way it can ever be solved—by disappearing. Wittgenstein asks: 'Where does our investigation get its importance from, since it seems only to destroy everything interesting, that is, all that is great and important?' And he answers: 'What we are destroying is nothing but houses of cards.'[4]

Of the two analogies, we might well find the positive and constructive spirit of the grammatical analogy the more attractive. Certainly I do. Still, we might feel that, at this stage at least, a certain advantage lies with the negative conception, if only because of the apparent modesty of the claim. For at least there is no doubt at all of the existence of perplexity, absurdity, and confusion in philosophy;

[4] Wittgenstein, *Philosophical Investigations*, § 118.

so there is no doubt, either, of the utility of a method which resolves, if it does, perplexity and confusion and dispels absurdity. And there is at least a certain prima-facie plausibility about the account offered of the genesis, and hence of the cure, of these disorders. As regards the positive suggestions or implications of the other analogy, on the other hand, there may well be doubt. Can there really be such a thing as an explanatory theory, or a set of connected theories, of our ordinary conceptual practice? In what terms, after all, should it be framed? No doubt there is such a thing as a systematic grammar of a language. But is there any reason for believing in the parallel suggested by the analogy? Is there any real reason for supposing that there is anything which deserves, even figuratively, to be called the grammar of our ordinary thinking? Perhaps we are just being encouraged to assume a structure, a possibility of theory, where there is nothing in fact but a loose assemblage of uses. Perhaps the reason why we cannot easily state the theory of our practice here is that there is nothing to state—nothing to do except point to the practice itself.

Here, then, is a thoroughgoing scepticism about the picture of the analytical philosopher's task as sketched in the grammatical analogy. As we go on, we shall see whether this scepticism can be countered. But even if one is not drawn to such a general scepticism regarding the analogy as I have just described; even if one feels an initial sympathy for it; yet one may well feel also a more specific doubt or reservation; of which I shall now speak.

It seems that the analogy might suffer from a certain serious defect or shortcoming. The attraction of the analogy rests on the contrast between the mastery of a practice, on the one hand, and, on the other, the ability to discern and state explicitly the principles which govern that practice. But surely, one might think, a distinction must here be drawn, between what might be called pre-theoretical or non-technical concepts on the one hand and essentially theoretical concepts on the other; between the common vocabulary of men and the specialist vocabularies of physicists, physiologists, economists, mathematicians, and biochemists. The grammatical analogy might have some application to the former, to the common vocabulary of men. But how can it have any application to the latter, to the special vocabularies of the special sciences? It is true that we master the ordinary notions of knowledge, perception, truth and meaning, personal identity and human emotions, action and responsibility, etc. without any theoretical training; hence true also that our ordinary thinking might have an unexplicit structure to be laid bare by the methods—whatever they may be—of philosophical analysis. But it is certainly not true that we master the key concepts of specialist disciplines without explicit theoretical instruction. There are countless books and crowds of teachers whose function is precisely to introduce us to the key concepts of their disciplines by means of explicit instruction. Are we then to conclude that philosophy, or at least modern analytical philosophy, has nothing to do with, and nothing to say about, such special sciences? If so, we must surely conclude also that it is a poor descendant of its distinguished ancestors; that it is, indeed, distinctly inferior to them. If one had suggested to Descartes that philosophy had nothing to do with physics; or to Aristotle that it had no relation to biology; or to Locke or Hume that what we now call empirical psychology had no part to play in it; or to Kant that philosophy had nothing to say about natural science in general—they would all have found such suggestions unintelligible. If philosophy is concerned with the structure of our thinking, it must surely be concerned with the structure of all our thinking, and not just with that of our least advanced and most commonplace thinking.

Clearly this criticism is a serious one. How might the defender of the grammatical analogy meet it? Well, we must certainly acknowledge that there is indeed a distinction between the theoretical concepts of, say, nuclear physics or economics and non-technical concepts like those of knowledge and identity; and we must acknowledge, too, that we learn to master the former, if we do, by a route of explicit theoretical instruction such as we do not follow, are not led along, in the case of the latter, the ordinary non-theoretical concepts. But we must ask what is the point and purpose of this route of explicit theoretical instruction. And the answer is that it is precisely to enable us to operate effectively *inside* the discipline concerned, *within* that discipline. The purpose is achieved if we become good economists, physicists, or whatnot; or, more modestly, if we are able to follow, with understanding, the reasonings and conclusions of good economists, physicists, etc. But there is no guarantee that theoretical instruction which achieves this purpose automatically confers on the instructed the ability to form an undistorted picture of the relation of the specialized discipline concerned to other human and intellectual concerns. But one of the principal philosophical drives is precisely to relate and connect our various intellectual and human concerns in some intelligible way.

The critic might well concede this point; but then add that it merely mentions another philosophical task which has no obvious connection with the general picture of philosophy presented by the grammatical analogy. That there is such a connection can be shown, however—as follows. The scientific specialist, let us suppose, is perfectly capable of explaining what he is doing with the special terms of his specialism. He has an explicit mastery, within the terms of his theory, of the special concepts of his theory. But he is also bound to use certain concepts which have a wider application than that of his specialism, concepts which are not really specialist concepts at all: for example, the concepts of explanation, demonstration, proof, conclusion, cause, event, fact, property, hypothesis, evidence, and theory itself—to mention only a few. Now in relation to these general concepts, as they figure in his discipline, the specialist may be in much the same position as we all are in relation to the pre-theoretical or non-technical concepts which we handle so easily in our ordinary intercourse with each other and the world. That is to say, the specialist may know perfectly well how to handle these concepts inside his discipline, i.e. be able to use them perfectly correctly there, without being able to say, in general, how he does it. Just as we, in our ordinary relations with things, have mastered a pre-theoretical practice without being necessarily able to state the principles of that practice, so he, the scientific specialist, may have mastered what we may call a theoretical practice without being able to state the principles of employment, within that practice, of terms which are not peculiar to it, terms which have a more general employment. Thus, for example, a historian may produce brilliant historical explanations without being able to say, in general, what counts as a historical explanation. A natural scientist may be fertile of brilliantly confirmed hypotheses but at a loss to give a general account of the confirmation of a scientific hypothesis, or even of the general nature of scientific hypotheses themselves. Again, a mathematician may discover and prove new mathematical truths without being able to say what are the distinctive characteristics of mathematical truth or of mathematical proof. So we have, besides history, the philosophy of history; besides natural science, the philosophy of science; besides mathematics, the philosophy of mathematics.

The point and relevance of these remarks should now be clear. I first mentioned the humanly felt need to relate our different intellectual concerns to each other and to our unspecialized concerns; or, if you like, to relate to each other our commonsense and non-theoretical picture of the world and our various abstract, theoretical, or specialized pictures of parts or aspects of the world; and I indicated that there is no reason to expect any particular kind of specialist to be particularly adept at this task, even where his own specialism is concerned. I next remarked that, even operating within his own specialism, a specialist was bound to employ concepts of more general application; and that, from the fact that he there employs them quite correctly, it by no means follows that he can give a clear and general account or explanation of what is characteristic of their employment in his specialism. But it is precisely in giving such explanations and in bringing out the differences and resemblances between them that one can bring out also the relations which exist between the different departments of our intellectual and human life. So the two tasks fall into one.

We see, then, how the question of the special sciences can, after all, be fitted into the framework of that positive conception of analysis presented by the grammatical analogy. But now, to balance the picture a little, let me note how a philosopher who favoured the negative, therapeutic conception of his role could present the considerations I have just been advancing in a very different fashion. All goes well, he might say—or well enough, aside from the ordinary difficulties of life and theory—so long as we are content simply to employ our ordinary concepts in their ordinary roles; to employ our technical concepts in their technical roles; and to employ the concepts which are common to different disciplines or to different disciplines and to daily life in the particular roles which they have in these different departments of their employment. Philosophical problems arise only because we are not satisfied to follow, or simply take note of, these employments; because we seek to unify, to theorize, to establish connections, in order to arrive at a comprehensive and unified conception of the world and our relation to it. Then our minds drift away from attention to our actual practice, from the role our concepts actually play in our lives; and we allow ourselves to be seduced by inappropriate models or pictures and to weave out of them bizarre and ultimately senseless theories, which are (to repeat the phrase of Wittgenstein's) 'nothing but houses of cards'. What is needed, then, is not a general explanatory theory, but a curative discipline which will remind us of the facts of use (remember, 'assemble reminders for a particular purpose') and perhaps also diagnose the sources of the philosophical illusions to which we are subject when our minds drift away from those facts.

It is easy to find some reinforcement for this negative view of the matter when we look at the history of philosophy and, in particular, the history of the relation of specialized disciplines to philosophy. I remarked earlier that there is no guarantee that competence within a specialized discipline carries with it automatically the ability to form an undistorted picture of the relation of the specialized discipline to other human and intellectual concerns. In fact the special competence may prove a special kind of handicap. If an eminent physicist, biologist, or even economist is moved to offer us a general picture of reality, a comprehensive account of how things are, it is not unlikely that his special discipline will be found occupying a central place in the picture, with other concerns subordinated to it or, as far as possible, reinterpreted in its terms.

There is, as it were, a tendency to intellectual imperialism on the part of, or on behalf of, different disciplines—so that now, say, physics, now biology, now psychology, now economics or sociology or anthropology—or even linguistics—will be felt to hold the master-key to general understanding; so that everything is to be understood in the light of physics, or biology, or the processes of economic production—or whatever else it may be. It goes almost without saying that any theory which claims to offer a general picture of reality, with everything in its place—but which is in fact constructed under the dominance of some such particular interest—that any such theory will be likely, indeed certain, to involve exaggeration and distortion. There may be a certain inevitability, and even a certain utility, in the production and diffusion of such theories. Inevitability, because the desire for a single master-key, which will open all the locks, seems natural to the species, a childish habit of mind of which we find it hard to break ourselves; and utility, because these dramatic, unified pictures of the world—these metaphysical images of reality—centred on a certain particular interest, may help to shake established habits of thought in a particular field of scientific investigation, and thus help to open the way for new developments or for the acceptance and diffusion of new developments.

An illustrious example of what I have in mind is provided by one of the greatest philosophers of the modern period: I mean, Descartes. I shall simplify, even caricature a little, his doctrine; but not, I hope, grossly. His world-picture could be seen as a form of conscious or unconscious propaganda in favour of a certain direction of development in the natural sciences. Mathematics, and in particular geometry, seemed to him to provide the model for scientific procedure. Although he recognized a place for experiment, he nevertheless thought that the deductive method, as one finds it in geometrical studies, was the fundamental method in science; and he thought that the subject-matter of all the physical sciences must be fundamentally the same as the subject-matter of geometry; and hence that, from the point of view of science in general, the only important characteristics of things in the physical world were the spatial characteristics which geometry studies.

It is not the mere holding of these beliefs which makes Descartes a metaphysician. It is rather the dramatic expression they receive in his doctrines about the essential nature of knowledge and existence. He offers a picture of the world in which the only realities, apart from God, are, on the one hand, purely material substance, of which the only real properties are spatial; and, on the other hand, pure thinking substances, or egos, whose essence consists in thought—

cogitatio—including, in particular, the ability to grasp self-evident axioms and their deductive consequences. So we have the subject-matter of geometry on the one hand; and minds capable of deductive or quasi-geometric reasoning on the other. True knowledge consists in the results of exercising this capability. Whatever else ordinarily passes either for reality or for knowledge finds itself, as it were, downgraded, given an inferior status. It is evident that we have here a fairly drastic revision of our ordinary scheme of things—a revision which naturally creates problems and calls for further explanations and adjustments. Thus we find Descartes teaching, for example, that it is only through confidence in God's veracity that we have reason to believe in the existence of material objects and, at the same time, that it is only through wilfulness that we ever come to believe what is false.

If I have treated the Cartesian picture too cavalierly, I must ask pardon of his shade and of you, my reader. In any case, Descartes is but one example—an illustrious one—of this kind of metaphysics; that is to say, of the production of a captivating and striking world-picture, dominated by a particular interest or a particular attitude, and correspondingly liable to distortion, to exaggeration, and, finally, even to incoherence. When we contemplate these systems, we may come to think that any attempt at positive systematic theory can only issue at best in some such distorting overall picture.

But must this be so? Must any such attempt at positive theory lead to nothing but such a result? That is the question. To find an answer to it, we must at least consider what form or forms a positive systematic theory might, or should, take.

✥ 2 ✥

Reduction or Connection?
Basic Concepts

WELL, then, what are the forms that a positive systematic analytical theory might take? Let us begin by returning to the word 'analysis' itself. As I earlier remarked, the most general implication of the name seems to be that of the resolution of something complex into elements and the exhibition of the ways in which the elements are related in the complex. What counts as an element will depend, naturally, on the kind of analysis that is in question. Chemical analysis stops with chemical elements. Physical analysis goes further. Syntactical analysis stops with morphemes, minimal meaningful word parts; whereas phonological analysis treats meaningful word parts as complex—its elements are phonemes. In each case we stop with items which are, from the point of view of the investigation in question, completely simple, the ultimate elements as regards that kind of analysis. Chemical elements are chemically simple; they lack chemical complexity. Morphemes have no grammatical structure. Phonemes do not themselves contain phonemes. And so on.

If we took this notion completely seriously for the case of conceptual analysis—analysis of ideas—we should conclude that our task was to find ideas that were completely simple, that were free from internal conceptual complexity; and then to demonstrate how the more or less complex ideas that are of interest to philosophers could be assembled by a kind of logical or conceptual construction out of these simple elements. The aim would be to get a clear grasp of complex meanings by reducing them, without remainder, to simple meanings. Thus baldly stated, this may seem a rather implausible project. And so it is. Nevertheless it, or some close relation of it, has been, and is, taken seriously. Even when not taken to the lengths I have just described, it continues to exercise a certain influence on the philosophical mind. I shall now try to explain just how this influence reveals itself.

When confronted with the task of giving a philosophical elucidation of some particular concept—say, for example, that of someone's *knowing* something to be the case or that of someone's *perceiving* some material object—we often attack it by trying to set out, in general terms, both the conditions which must be satisfied if the concept is to be correctly applied and the conditions which are such that the concept must be correctly applicable if those conditions are satisfied. That is to say, in our jargon, we try to ascertain the necessary and sufficient conditions of the correct application of the concept.

We may, and usually do, set about this style of analysis in a relatively modest spirit. That is, we do not aim at including only concepts which are themselves absolutely simple (whatever they may be!) in our statement of necessary and sufficient conditions for the application of a given concept. We may, for example, find that the concept of *belief* figures as an element in our analysis of the concept of *knowledge* and be quite content with this situation even though we also think that the concept of belief requires, and is capable of, analysis. But that we may regard as a problem for another day or another chapter.

So far, then, there seems no reason to think that the philosopher in practice operates at all with the reductive model or picture of analysis which I have sketched—the model in which the conception of the simple, at least as the ideal limit of analysis, plays an essential part. But there is an element of the situation which suggests that the model really does have a certain power over him. For there is a certain form of words which the analytical philosopher hates to hear and which his opponent in argument, also an analytical philosopher, delights to pronounce: viz. the words, 'Your analysis is circular'. This means, of course, that included in the elements of his analysis, though perhaps covertly included and only to be revealed by further steps of the same kind, is the very concept which the philosopher is claiming to analyse.

Now why should this formula be felt to be so damaging? Well, of course, the formula 'Your analysis is circular, it suffers from circularity' really is damaging, indeed fatally damaging, to the pretended analysis if we are thinking in terms of that model of analysis which represents it as a kind of dismantling of a complex structure into simpler elements, a process which terminates only when you reach pieces which cannot be further dismantled; for this process has not even begun if one of the alleged pieces turns out to be, or to contain, the very thing, the very concept, that was to be dismantled.

But now let us consider a quite different model of philosophical analysis. This new model I am going to declare more realistic and more fertile than the one just discussed. (It might be thought better to use the word 'elucidation' rather than 'analysis', since the latter so strongly suggests the dismantling model; but I shall stick to 'analysis' all the same, since it is consecrated by usage and since it has, in any case, a more comprehensive sense than that of which I have spoken.) Let us abandon the notion of perfect simplicity in concepts; let us abandon even the notion that analysis must always be in the direction of greater simplicity. Let us imagine, instead, the model of an elaborate network, a system, of connected items, concepts, such that the function of each item, each concept, could, from the philosophical point of view, be properly understood only by grasping its connections with the others, its place in the system— perhaps better still, the picture of a set of interlocking systems of such a kind. If this becomes our model, then there will be no reason to be worried if, in the process of tracing connections from one point to another of the network, we find ourselves returning to, or passing through, our starting-point. We might find, for example, that we could not fully elucidate the concept of knowledge without reference to the concept of sense perception; and that we could not explain all the features of the concept of sense perception without reference to the concept of knowledge. But this might be an unworrying and unsurprising fact. So the general charge of circularity would lose its sting, for we might have moved in a wide, revealing, and illuminating circle. This is not to say that the charge of circularity would lose its sting in every case. Some circles are too small and we move in them unawares, thinking we have established a revealing connection when we have not. But it would be a matter for judgement to say when the charge was damaging and when it was not.

I have already remarked that the programme of reductive or atomistic analysis, according to which the limits of analysis were to be absolutely simple concepts or meanings—that this programme seemed distinctly implausible. More often, at least in the British empiricist tradition, it has not been concepts exactly that have been seen as the candidate atoms, the simple elements of analysis, but rather those fleeting items of subjective experience, or those parts of such items, which David Hume called 'simple impressions'; and also those supposed copies of these, presented in imagination or memory, which he called 'simple ideas'. These were the irreducible elements in terms of which Hume proposed to explain our picture of the world. It seems too that these were the atoms of that logical atomism to which Lord Russell adhered towards the end of the first quarter of this century. I shall have more to say later about this school of philosophical analysis. But the point that I want to make now is different. It is that any philosopher who believes in the atomic or simple elements of reductive analysis, however he conceives them, will obviously view these simple elements in a special light. He will view them as basic to our whole conceptual structure, to our entire conception of the world; for everything else is to be explained in terms of them, while they are not to be explained in terms of anything else. They will be conceptually ultimate or enjoy absolute conceptual priority. They will be absolutely fundamental in our scheme of things.

Now these notions—of the *ultimate*, the *basic*, of that which enjoys *absolute priority* or is *absolutely fundamental* in our scheme, or schemes, of things—these are obviously appealing. They are among the notions which initially attract us to philosophy. So we may ask: is it only the reductive style of analytical philosophy, with its commitment to atoms of analysis, which allows us to make use of these fascinating notions? Must we eschew these fascinating notions altogether if we find more realistic the alternative model I have sketched: the model of tracing connections in a system without hope of being able to dismantle or reduce the concepts we examine to other and simpler concepts? If this is the model we prefer—we might call it the connective model to contrast it with the reductive or atomistic model—must we then give up the notion of what is fundamental from the conceptual point of view? I think not. In saying that, of course, I expose myself to the question: where, then, are we to look for the basic concepts, once we have given up reliance, or exclusive reliance, on the model of reductive definition?

Well, here is one pointer. I remarked earlier that we are introduced to the technical concepts of the special disciplines by way of explicit instruction in the elements of economics, physics, or whatever it may be. In what terms does such instruction proceed? It doesn't take place in an intellectual vacuum. Connections must be made with the conceptual equipment which the learners already possess. Our mastery of the concepts of the specialized disciplines must somehow be made to grow out of the conceptual materials we have mastered already. We have no need to enquire exactly how this is done—by what processes of refinement, extension, or analogy—though we can be pretty sure that it is not simply a matter of strictly defining new theoretical concepts in terms of pre-theoretical concepts. For the point I am making is an extremely simple one: that the acquisition of the theoretical concepts of the special disciplines presupposes and rests upon the possession of the pre-theoretical concepts of ordinary life. Certainly one can do things with the refined (specialized) instruments which one could not do with the blunt (common) instruments. But the refined instruments are available only because the blunt (or relatively blunt) instruments were there before them.

Here, then, is one way in which concepts can be ordered in respect of priority: the ability to operate with one set of concepts may presuppose the ability to operate with another set, and not vice versa. In this case we may say that the presupposed concepts are conceptually prior to the presupposing concepts; which suggests, according to what I have just said, that it is among the concepts employed in ordinary non-technical discourse and not among those

employed only in specialized technical discourse that the philosophically basic concepts—if indeed there really are such things—are to be
found.

But the concepts of ordinary non-technical discourse are so
numerous and so heterogeneous! If we were to make a random list of
such concepts as they came into our heads, they would mostly be
such that it would seem prima facie absurd to claim for them the
special status of being philosophically fundamental. Here, for
example, is a random selection: car, guitar, concert, ambassador,
snow, pebble, street, cat. If one asks why it would seem absurd to
represent any of these as basic or fundamental, the answers are not
far to seek. First, it seems utterly contingent, an accident of nature
and society, that we have any use for such concepts. It is easy to
imagine forms of life and experience in which they would have no
place. Indeed no effort of imagination is necessary: it is enough to
think of other periods of history or of other regions of the world. So
these concepts are not merely contingent; they are, one might say,
merely provincial. Again, some at least of such common concepts are
capable of being reductively defined, easily dismantled without
remainder or circularity into more general ideas; and this would
seem to disqualify them in anybody's eyes, and not merely in those
of the reductive or dismantling analyst, for the status of fundamental
or basic concepts. And, finally, these concepts, whether easily
dismantled or not, are surely insufficiently general; they are much
too specific.

If we stand these answers on their heads, it seems that we should
be looking for concepts which are highly general; which are non-
dismantlable (i.e. which resist reductive definition); and which are
non-contingent. Non-contingency is a difficult notion which I shall
leave on one side for a moment. Of non-dismantlability or
irreducibility I have already said something: it is here of the greatest
importance to remember that 'irreducible' does not mean or imply
'simple'. A concept may be complex, in the sense that its
philosophical elucidation requires the establishing of its connections
with other concepts, and yet at the same time irreducible, in the
sense that it cannot be defined away, without circularity, in terms of

those other concepts to which it is necessarily related. What, then, of the third requirement, that of generality?

Well, some of those common concepts which I just now listed—car, pebble, guitar—though lacking in generality themselves, have in common, and share with very many other non-technical concepts as well, a feature of very high generality indeed: viz., that they are all concepts of material objects or, to use the older philosophical term, of *bodies*. Might not the concept of body, of material object, be a good example of a candidate for the role of basic concept?

It might seem that there is a difficulty here. I just now suggested that the natural hunting-ground for basic concepts—if there were such things—was ordinary non-technical discourse. But though the word 'body' is an ordinary enough word, the philosopher's use of it is really not quite ordinary. We should not ordinarily call a chair or a mountain a 'body'. We do not ordinarily have occasion to use an expression of quite such general application as the philosopher makes, or used to make, of this word. But this difficulty is easily resolved. If a philosopher claimed that the concept of 'body' was basic in our conceptual structure, his claim could be understood as a kind of shorthand for the claim that it was a basic feature of our conceptual structure that it contained a range of concepts of a certain general type, namely, concepts of different kinds of body; and he could maintain this consistently with admitting that we ordinarily had no occasion to make use of so comprehensive a classification.

This is a point of some importance, for we often find it happens that the analytical philosopher uses words which belong to common discourse in senses rather different from, and wider than, those that they ordinarily possess; and that he does this often with the same purpose as that just illustrated, viz. that of making more general classifications than we ordinarily have occasion to make. This is true, for example, of his use of the words 'perceive' and 'perception'; of the words 'particular' and 'universal'; of the words 'property' and 'proposition'. This does not mean that he is not still concerned with our ordinary conceptual apparatus, our ordinary equipment of ideas. That ordinary equipment still remains his subject. Only he is talking about it at a higher level of generality than that at which we habitually find ourselves. What he says at that level is compatible with a great variety of ways in which the general features he is concerned with are realized or represented in the conceptual equipment which satisfies our ordinary needs.

Now of course I have not, in the foregoing, been arguing—though I shall do so later—that the concept of body is in fact a basic or fundamental concept in the sense we are concerned with. I have just adduced it as an illustration of one kind of direction in which the search for highly general and basic features of our conceptual structure might go. That is to say, we might sometimes find such a feature to consist in the fact of our employment of a range of more specific concepts which belong to a certain general type, a type of which, in our ordinary business with the world, we have little occasion to form a distinct conception. But of course we may also expect to find that there are other concepts which occur quite ordinarily in daily use and which themselves have the character of basic concepts—for example, the concepts of *time*, of *change*, of *truth*, of *identity*, of *knowledge*.

However, we were looking, not just for possible examples, but for a general sense which we could give to the notion of 'the basic' in connection with the alternative model I proposed for philosophical analysis—the model of tracing connections in a system rather than reducing the complex to simple, or simpler, elements. Putting together the various considerations we now have before us, we might arrive at something like the following sufficiently vague formula:

A concept or concept-type is basic in the relevant sense if it is one of a set of general, pervasive, and ultimately irreducible concepts or concept-types which together form a structure—a structure which constitutes the framework of our ordinary thought and talk and which is presupposed by the various specialist or advanced disciplines that contribute, in their diverse ways, to our total picture of the world.

Evidently this is not a self-explanatory formula. Many notions in it call for further elucidation—e.g. those of connection, ultimate irreducibility, presupposition—which I hope they will receive, if only by way of illustration, as we go on. Meanwhile it will serve.

What I want next to mention is the possibility of a rather stronger conception of basic conceptual structure than that which I have just outlined. And here there come into prominence those notions of contingency and non-contingency which I mentioned earlier and set on one side. I remarked then that one of the reasons we might have for counting as prima facie absurd any suggestion that such concepts as 'car', 'guitar', 'concert', etc. had the special philosophical interest that would attach to basic concepts was that it seemed an utterly contingent matter that we in fact had any use for such concepts. But what are the limits of contingency, and how are they drawn? Suppose a philosopher makes a plausible shot at describing what he claims to be the general structure of ideas underlying our common discourse and presupposed by our special enquiries. Might not the question be raised whether it is not a purely contingent, accidental matter that we operate with such a structure of ideas as he describes?

The question can be understood in at least two ways, one of which leads to no interesting issue. It might be said: every proposition is contingent if its negation generates no self-contradiction in strict logic, even if its negation is obviously false and even if the very fact of issuing it shows it to be false. So it is contingent in this sense that any sentient and thinking beings exist at all, and hence it is contingent that any concepts find any employment at all; although no one can deny the existence of such beings and the employment of concepts without thereby showing his denial to be false.

But the question can also be understood in a much more interesting, though less definite, sense. From within the scheme of ideas which we actually have, we can readily enough make sense of the suggestion that our experience might have been such that a certain quite pervasive concept or range of concepts of ordinary life had no part at all to play—that we would indeed have been incapable of framing concepts of that particular kind. The concept of colour, indeed of visual experience in general, seems to be an example of this. That is to say, we can, or it seems that we can, frame a perfectly intelligible and coherent conception of a type of experience from which this feature, and hence the concept of this feature, would be completely absent. The conception of a colourless world—or of experience of the world as colourless—is not just not self-contradictory, it is intelligible in a much stronger sense. We do not, in entertaining it, in imaginatively making it ours, feel our grip on the conception of ourselves as experiencing and thinking beings in any way loosened or imperilled. The same thing can be said of the general concept of sound. (The existence of the blind and the deaf is perhaps proof enough of this.) Nevertheless it seems improbable that there are no limits to this kind of conceptual stripping down of our experience—limits beyond which the very conception of experience itself would be lost. That is to say, it seems probable that there are some structural features of our experience which are essential to any conception (comprehensible to us) of the experience of self-conscious beings.

Suppose there are indeed such limits—limits determining the minimum structure which we can find intelligible as a possible structure of experience. Then the elements of this structure, and the structure itself, will be basic in a stronger sense than that which we have considered previously. For they will be—and here we find the opposition to the notion of contingency which we were seeking— they will be *necessary* features of any conception of experience which we can make intelligible to ourselves, and hence the concepts of these features will be, in just this sense, necessary concepts, non-contingent elements of our conceptual structure. Of all the great philosophers it was, of course, Immanuel Kant who made the most serious and determined effort to establish a certain minimal conceptual structure as necessary. He tried to etablish, one might say, the lower limits of sense. Some other philosophers have perhaps sometimes strayed below those limits; and this might particularly be said of some of those who were, in one way or another, dominated by an atomistic conception of analysis.

(I should perhaps add parenthetically that straying below the limits is not the only way in which philosophers can go, and have gone, beyond the bounds of sense. There is an upper as well as a lower bound. Significance can wither, or nonsense flourish, as a result of conceptual excess as well as a result of conceptual deficiency; and perhaps conceptual over-indulgence is more common than conceptual starvation. Kant himself sets an upper bound as well as a lower bound.)

We have then two conceptions of basic conceptual structures—

two conceptions of which one is stronger, more demanding, than the other, since it requires its basic structural elements to be necessary or non-contingent. We need not cultivate either of these conceptions to the exclusion of the other. Questions arise about both. In particular the stronger conception is exposed to a kind of scepticism. By what kind of argument could it be shown that any concept or complex of concepts had the character of necessity envisaged in that conception? The question is obviously a serious one. But the interest and importance of the analytical enterprise are not seriously diminished if we cannot find a satisfactory answer to it. For there always remains the other conception, the less demanding one; and to arrive at a clear understanding of the most general features of our conceptual structure, as it exists in fact—whether or not it is possible to demonstrate the necessity of those features—is a sufficient task for any philosopher, however ambitious. If, then, one finds oneself forced to abandon the stronger conception of fundamental structure—and I do not say that one must or will—one can settle, without dismay, for the less strong.

But now I should remind you of another kind of scepticism to which even this more modest conception may be exposed. In the course of my first chapter I contrasted the positive conception of analysis, illustrated by the analogy of grammar, with the negative or anti-theoretical conception, favoured by the extreme adherents—if there are any—of the analogy of therapy. Evidently the latter can be expected to look with a fairly cold eye on the project of bringing to light underlying conceptual structure. For the message is: don't look for anything underlying. Look at the concepts which puzzle you actually in use in the various human concerns ('forms of life' in Wittgenstein's phrase) which give them their whole significance. Get a clear view of *that*—admittedly not an easy thing to do—and then you will be free. Don't try for a general theory. That is the message.

But one could say: isn't this doctrine, in a slightly paradoxical way, itself a doctrine about what is basic from the philosophical point of view, viz. 'forms of life'? Indeed Wittgenstein himself says: 'What *has to be accepted—the given*—is, so one could say—forms of life.'[1]

[1] *Philosophical Investigations*, II. xi. 226.

And now one is tempted to ask: does this mean that one can say nothing at all about the *connections* between forms of life? It would be hard to give a good reason for that. So let us leave this kind of scepticism aside.

❦ 3 ❦

Moore and Quine

WHAT I have said so far about conceptual analysis has been of a fairly loose and schematic character. Now, by way of a check on it all, I wish to draw attention to another answer to the question, 'What is philosophy'—an answer given more than seventy years ago by one of the founding fathers of modern analytical philosophy. The philosopher in question is George Edward Moore, whose name, I think, is not very often mentioned in Continental Europe and whose work has rather gone out of fashion even in English-speaking countries. (So much the worse, one may add, for fashion—given that, more than any other philosopher of our century, Moore took pains to avoid rhetoric and obscurity and to say nothing which was not absolutely clear.) His answer to the question, 'What is philosophy?', may at first seem rather different from the one I have sketched; but I shall try to indicate how and why the two answers in the end begin to approximate to one another. The question itself is the title of the first chapter of his book, *Some Main Problems in Philosophy*, a book which was not published until 1953, but which consists of a series of lectures given in London in 1910 and 1911. On the first page he says the following:

To begin with, then, it seems to me that the most important and interesting thing which philosophers have tried to do is no less than this; namely: To give a general description of the whole of the *Universe*, mentioning all the most important kinds of things which we *know* to be in it, considering how far it is likely that there are in it important kinds of things which we do not absolutely *know* to be in it and also considering the most important ways in which these various kinds of things are related to each other. I will call all this for short 'Giving a general description of the *whole* Universe'; and hence will say that the first and most important problem of philosophy is: To give a general description of the *whole* Universe.

Moore spends a great deal, indeed most, of the rest of the chapter doing two things: first, setting out what he calls the view of Common Sense on this matter, i.e. on the question what the most important kinds of things that we know to be in the universe are etc.; and, second, contrasting this view with various views which have been held by philosophers who have either added to, or subtracted from, the Common Sense answer or who have done both at once. In addition he remarks, justly enough, that philosophers who have set about this task of giving a general description of the universe have not generally thought it sufficient to state their *opinion* on this question; they have also *argued* in favour of their views and have often sought to refute, i.e. have argued against, contrary views. So we have the notion, not just of a description, but of an argued description. Moore also adds that many philosophers have tried to *define* those great classes of things which they think to be the most important that there are or that we know there to be; and perhaps, though this is not quite clear, he thinks this task of defining those great classes is at least part of what he refers to, in the passage I quoted, as 'considering the most important ways in which these various kinds of things are related'; though, perhaps again, we may find in this talk of definition a suggestion, at least, of the dismantling type of analysis.

Of all the problems and tasks mentioned so far Moore says that they belong to that department of philosophy which is called Metaphysics. But I hardly think he would dissent if one here suggested another name, equally appropriate, viz. Ontology. This name is appropriate because, as we have seen, the question Moore here has in mind is the question concerning what the most important kinds of things are that *are*, or that *exist*, or that it is known or thought likely that there *are* or that *exist*; and, further, how they are related to each other or how they are to be defined. And these questions, as treated by philosophers, are traditionally called ontological questions.

In the very few pages of this chapter which remain Moore remarks that there are other questions which have an obvious bearing on the ontological questions which he regards as the most important; though these questions may also be said to belong to other departments of philosophy. The questions he goes on to mention are, first, questions about the nature and foundations of knowledge—epistemological questions; and with these he associates, on the one hand, questions in the philosophy of mind or philosophical psychology and, on the other hand, questions he wants to assign to another department of philosophy, which he calls Logic. This last department includes, besides formal logic, general questions about the nature of truth, about grounds, evidence, proof; and perhaps we should assign to it also all the questions which now go under the head of philosophy of language. Finally Moore mentions one more department, namely Ethics; but, having already published *Principia Ethica*, he has nothing more to say about ethics in the course of the book; and it is a subject on which I too propose to remain largely silent in these pages.

Is it true that, ethics apart, philosophy can be divided into, say, three great departments bearing those impressive names, Ontology, Epistemology, Logic? Some would say that any such division is misleading, even if we add that the three departments are intimately connected with each other. And perhaps it can mislead. But I think also that it can be useful to bear in mind these names and their significance when we try to fill out our picture of conceptual analysis, to supply it with more substance and more detail.

But we have a more immediate issue to face. Moore says, as we have seen, that the philosopher's main task is that of answering the metaphysical or ontological question: what are the most important kinds of things that exist, or are known to exist, and how are they related? Two very obvious questions arise for us about this question of Moore's. First, what does Moore mean by 'important' when he talks of the most important kinds of thing that exist? And, second, how, if at all, is this talk of the most important kinds of things that exist related to all that I have said so far in these pages, where I have not, it seems, confronted any such question, but have spoken only of concepts and conceptual structures and conceptual analysis?

If we take the word 'important' by itself, we do not get very far.

Ask a man what he regards as the most important things that exist. You may get all sorts of replies. One man may say: 'To me personal relations are the most important thing in the world'; and another: 'For me, it's music.' Yet another might say: 'Those are just personal, human preferences. What is really important is the mechanism of ecological balance in Nature, on which all else depends.' To which a biologist might reply: 'Something of more fundamental importance still is the structure of the DNA molecule, on which all life depends.' And then the physicist might say: 'On this scale, I win; for I study the structure and properties of the ultimate physical particles of which all matter is composed and on which, consequently, every-thing whatever depends.'

It is clear, I hope, that there is really no sense in asking 'What are the most important kinds of things there are?' as a perfectly general question, divorced from any background of assumption or any specification of the type of interest or the type of enquiry concerned. Nevertheless, we can begin to understand what Moore really means by 'important' in the present context, what the relevant criteria of importance are, by considering the view he ascribes to Common Sense on the question he poses. The Common Sense view, as he calls it, mentions, first and foremost, material or physical objects and, second, acts or states of consciousness as among the most important kinds of *things* there are; and, moreover, mentions the fact that at least the first of these kinds of things are in space and both of these kinds of things are in time as among the most important kinds of *facts* about these most important kinds of things. Now, one of the first things that must strike us about this list of kinds of thing and of fact is their very high degree of generality and comprehensiveness. The classifications, 'physical object' and 'act or state of conscious-ness' are of an extreme generality, as is the fact that items falling under these classifications are spatial and temporal, or at least temporal, items. So it seems that we could explain at least part of Moore's meaning in his account of the principal task of philosophy by simply replacing the word 'important' by the word 'general' throughout that account.

Now here is a point of contact with the account I have given of the activity of the philosopher who is concerned with conceptual structures, and, in particular, with that sort of ordering of concepts which would permit him to speak of certain among them as basic or fundamental; for generality was precisely one of the features which were to characterize basic concepts. Yet, even if there is a point of contact, it seems that there is still a substantial difference: the difference, already mentioned, that where Moore speaks of the most general kinds of *things that exist* in the universe, I have spoken of the most general concepts or concept-types which form part of a scheme or structure of ideas or concepts which we employ in *thinking and talking* about things in the universe. But I want first to say that this difference, though real, is not as great as it may look; and, second, to suggest that, in so far as the difference is real, there is reason to prefer this conceptual style of talking. By talking about our conceptual structure, the structure of our thought about the world, rather than, as it were, directly about the world, we keep a firmer grasp of our own philosophical procedure, a clearer understanding of what we are about.

The difference, then, is not quite so great as it seems. It is admitted that there are concepts and concept-types of high generality which are thoroughly pervasive of our thought and talk about the world, which are indeed such that there is almost no slice of such thought or talk which does not exemplify or presuppose them. Moore's two examples—the concepts of material objects and states of consciousness—will serve to illustrate the point. In so far as these are concepts of kinds of thing, it is quite inconceivable that these concepts should have this pervasive or universal employment unless we took it for granted that there were, or existed, in the world things to which those concepts, or concepts of those concept-types, applied. So the question: 'What are our most general concepts, or types of concept, of things?' and the question: 'What are the most general types of thing we take there to *be*, or *exist*?' really come to the same thing.

But here an obvious objection arises. Someone will say: 'You seem to have missed the whole point of Moore's chapter. You seem to be saying that the fact that certain concepts or concept-types are very general and very pervasive of our thought and discourse carries certain ontological implications. And no doubt this is right if by 'ontological implications' here is meant implications about the very general types of thing which we *take* to exist or, as Moore puts it, to be in the universe. But isn't Moore's point that the prime task of the philosopher is to say not just what we ordinarily take to be the case in this matter, not just what our ordinary ontological assumptions are, but whether those assumptions are true or whether we know them to be true. And he points out, doesn't he, that the view of Common Sense on this matter has been challenged by some philosophers—for example, by those who have denied the existence of material bodies in space. So surely there is a real and important difference between the question: "What are the most general types of thing that exist and how are they related?" and the question: "What are our most general and pervasive concepts, or types of concepts, of things and how are they related?" The answer to the second question may indeed carry implications about our normal beliefs or assumptions regarding the answer to the first question. But the first question is, among other things, the question whether those beliefs or assumptions are true and known to be true.'

There are several possible replies to this objection, of varying degrees of toughness. I shall not give any of the tough replies, but instead a rather mild one. The mild reply goes like this. Surely it is a fact that we must give great weight to, that the pervasiveness and generality of certain concepts or concept-types carries ontological implications in the undisputed sense; that is, implications about what we ordinarily and quite generally *take* to exist. Given all the warnings we have noticed about how philosophical paradox and confusion may arise from failure to take account of how our concepts actually function in use, it would surely be reasonable to get a clear grasp of how they do function before trying to evaluate the reasons which some philosophers might have given for challenging our general accepted working ontology. In giving any such reasons, moreover, the challenging philosopher must start from somewhere; he must start from some point inside our existing equipment of ideas. Perhaps he starts from some abstract considerations about existence and identity, or unity and plurality; perhaps from considerations about the nature of knowledge or experience or consciousness. But in any case we shall be better able to evaluate his reasons if we have a clear picture of how those concepts which form his starting-point actually work in relation to the rest of our conceptual equipment.

This mild response leads us back to the position we had reached before Moore was brought on the scene. We reconstrue, at least provisionally, what he calls the philosopher's main task—the metaphysical task—as that of answering the question: what are the most general concepts or categories in terms of which we organize our thought about, our experience of, the world? And how are they related in the total structure of our thought? In answering this question, it seems we must incidentally answer the question in its most general form, of how we actually conceive the world to be, or what our basic ontology (our working ontology) actually is. But also, reconstruing what Moore calls the philosopher's main task in these terms will help us better to appreciate the relations between the members of that supposed departmental trio: ontology, logic, and epistemology. We shall see that the general theory of being (ontology), the general theory of knowledge (epistemology), and the general theory of the proposition, of what is true or false (logic) are but three aspects of one unified enquiry. How is that assertion to be demonstrated? This is the task to which I shall set myself in the chapters which follow—beginning with the remainder of this one.

First, then, as to logic. What can logic, formal logic, have to do with the enquiry into our general framework or structure of concepts and categories? Well, concepts are for use, not for ornament. The use of concepts, Kant said, is in judgement: that is to say, in consciously forming or holding a belief about what is the case. Not the only use. We use concepts whenever we form a plan or intention, entertain a wish, or are conscious of a desire. But there is neither plan nor desire without belief. So the fundamental use of concepts, the use which concerns us here, is the use we make of them when we consciously form a judgement or hold a belief about what is or has been or will be the case in the world, in fact. Some of the older logicians used to say that logic was the study of the general forms of judgement and of the relations of deductive dependence or independence which held between them. This description, though nearly enough correct, calls for a slight amendment. It is better to say that logic is the study of the general forms of the *proposition* and of *their* relations of logical dependence and independence. What is the difference? In the earlier phase of his philosophical career Wittgenstein wrote, in the *Tractatus Logico-Philosophicus*, the following sentence: 'The completely general form of *all* propositions is: This is how things are.'[1] Well, we can certainly judge or believe that this is how things are, that things are thus-and-so. But we can also doubt or wonder whether things are thus-and-so; or we can judge that *if* things are thus-and-so, then such-and-such is the case— without actually judging that things are thus-and-so. The *proposition* that things are thus-and-so will figure equally in all these situations, though only in the first will it figure as a judgement. So general or formal logic takes a step in abstraction from particular propositional attitudes (as they are called) of believing, doubting, supposing, hoping, etc., and studies the general forms of whatever may be believed or doubted or hypothesized, and so on; that is it studies the general forms of the proposition and their relations. The links between propositions and propositional attitudes are not broken. The essential property of the proposition is to be the bearer, or potential bearer, of a truth value, to be capable of being true or false; and when we talk of the relations of logical dependence or independence between propositions, we are talking of certain relations of dependence or independence as regards truth value. But only what is capable of being believed, doubted, hypothesized, supposed, etc. is capable of having a truth value.

The life of the concept, then, is in the proposition and logic studies the general forms of the proposition and hence the general forms of all our beliefs about the world. But what does this mean? In particular, how big a step in abstraction is represented by that phrase 'the general forms of the proposition'? The answer is, or seems to be: a simply enormous step. For logic, it is said, studies the *forms* of the proposition, hence the *forms* of thought, in total abstraction from its subject-matter, from the subject-matter of thought; hence, it seems, in total abstraction even from such very general concepts and categories as Moore mentions as entering into our commonsense

---

[1] *Tractatus Logico-Philosophicus*, 4. 5.

ontology—concepts of material things, of states of consciousness, or Space and Time. So, one may ask, what bearing can formal logic have on metaphysical enquiries? What possible relation can it have to ontology? And it may begin to look as if the only answer is: none.

Yet one thing is quite certain: that the general thought of an intimate connection between logic and ontology or metaphysics has run like a thread, one of many threads, right through the history of philosophy, from Aristotle to the present. One can mention, for example, Aristotle himself, Leibniz, Kant, Frege, Russell, Wittgenstein, and, in our own day, Quine—not to speak of the scholastic philosophers of the Middle Ages. Kant tried to make this connection in a singularly direct way. Having listed the forms of propositions, according, more or less, to the contemporary conception of logic, he asked what concepts must have application to the world of our experience for it to be possible for objectively true judgements to be framed in the forms he distinguished. It is true that, in order to make any real advance, he had to appeal to other considerations which took him beyond pure formal logic. (Later on we shall find ourselves in the same situation in this respect.) But logic supplied him, as it will supply us, with a point of departure. Wittgenstein, in the days of the *Tractatus*, seems to have greatly overestimated the power of logic to yield direct ontological conclusions. He came to the surprising conclusion that the ultimate constituents of the world must be such that the simplest propositions about them must all be completely independent of each other; that no conclusion about the truth or falsity of any such proposition could be drawn from the truth or falsity of any other. This logico-ontological conclusion has come to seem unwarranted, even bizarre.

What, then, does logic offer us, and how should the connection be made with metaphysics and ontology? There might seem to be another initial difficulty here, in that logic is a subject with a history, stretching from the syllogistic of Aristotle to the modern classical or standard logic of Frege and Russell and variants on the latter. But we must not make too much of this. For there are certain fundamental logical notions which are to be found, more or less adequately represented, in anything we could recognize as a more or less adequate system of logic. So let us take the dominant current logic—

standard or classical logic—as our guide. It is certainly more powerful and comprehensive than anything that has preceded it; and as for its variants, they are precisely that, variants on *it*; and I shall neglect them.

Taking the current dominant logic as our guide has also the practical advantage that some at least, perhaps many, of my readers will be perfectly well acquainted with the fundamental notions of propositional and first-order predicate logic. So I shall run very sketchily over its content, emphasizing just the main features I shall need to refer to later. The most elementary part of our logic is, of course, the propositional calculus or the logic of truth-functional composition. I shall not linger on it. It simply exploits the essential feature of propositions already noted, namely that they are bearers of truth value and may have only one of the two incompatible truth values, true and false—it simply exploits this feature in order to introduce particles (or propositional connectives, as they are called) which are used to frame compound propositions of which the truth values are completely determined, in different ways, by the truth values of the propositions of which they are compounded. This in turn obviously generates further relations of logical dependence between the compound propositions thus formed. But this part of logic, taken by itself, has no concern with the internal structure of the uncompounded propositions which enter into its compounds. It has nothing to say about what we might call the *form of the content* of logically simple propositions; and hence it has nothing to teach us of an ontological order.

Let us turn, then, to consider the general forms of the simplest propositions recognized in our logic, the internal structure of atomic propositions, as we may call them. Here our logic provides for a quite fundamental duality, a fundamental distinction. It is easy enough to say how this distinction or duality is represented in the schemata or formulae of logic. It is not so easy to say clearly and generally what it is exactly that is thus represented. In logical schemata we represent the distinction in question by the distinction between predicate letters (capitals) and individual variables (small letters). Thus we give the general *forms* of logically simple or atomic propositions by writing a *single predicate letter* in concatenation with *one or more individual variables.* To fill these forms in such a way as to obtain actual examples of propositions, we must replace the predicate letter with a predicate expression (a verb or a verb phrase) and we must replace the individual variables by appropriate definite singular substantives, that is, by proper names, pronouns, or definite descriptions. Consider, for example, the following simple sentences: 'John is asleep', 'John loves Mary', 'John gives Fido to Mary'; or '2 is prime', '9 is greater than 7', '7 is between 5 and 9'. In such examples the distinction between the two sorts of expression stands out clearly: we have on the one hand singular substantive expressions—'definite singular terms'—such as 'John', 'Mary', '2', '7', etc., and on the other hand predicative verbs or verb phrases such as 'is asleep', 'loves', 'is prime', 'is greater than', etc. Equally, perhaps, we may find it natural to distinguish two sorts of role played respectively by these two sorts of expression in the production of the unified thing, the proposition: the role of reference on the one hand, played by the substantive expressions, and the role of predication on the other hand, played, evidently, by the predicative expressions.

We have, then, a distinction of types of expression and a distinction of types of role; or, in other words, a grammatical distinction and a functional distinction. The question is whether we can associate with these distinctions yet another, this time of an ontological order. It would seem that, in order to do so, it would be necessary to enquire into the kinds of things that these two kinds of expression respectively represent or stand for. And here we might make a tentative start by saying that the definite singular substantives refer to individuals or objects; while the predicate expressions signify or represent general concepts or properties or relations.

This last distinction, between individual on the one hand and general property or relation on the other begins to look like an ontological distinction. But we should recognize that these words may mislead us. So far all that we are entitled to understand by 'individual' or 'object' is 'item specified by a name or other definite singular term in a simple proposition'; and, so far as we can tell on purely formal or grammatical grounds, there may be no restriction whatever on the kinds of item which can be thus specified. In this sense, then, individuals may include what we ordinarily call properties—as when we say, for example, 'Courage is a virtue'—or abstract branches of study, as when we say 'Logic was founded by Aristotle'. It remains to be seen whether or not we should accept an ontology of objects which includes everything our discourse treats as an individual in the sense concerned.

Now of course our thought is not limited to simple singular propositions and propositions compounded of these with the aid of the particles of the propositional calculus. We are capable of thinking of specific concepts as applying or not applying in various combinations without always specifying in our thought particular individual items to which they apply or do not apply. In other words we are capable of explicitly general thinking. And this fact too must be reflected in any logic worthy of the name. In our standard logic it is reflected by the device of quantification binding individual variables. The expressions for the concepts which enter as predicates into such thoughts replace, as before, the predicate letters in the atomic schemata or their compounds; but the individual variables, instead of being replaced by, say, names of individual items of which the concept is predicated, are brought under the control of quantifiers, i.e. expressions signifying one or another kind of generality. The two quantifiers recognized in our logic correspond roughly to the expressions 'some' and 'every'. Thus, besides the simple singular proposition, 'John sleeps', we have the general proposition, 'Someone sleeps', written in the logical notation as 'For some value of x, x sleeps'. Beside the singular compound proposition, 'If John sleeps, he dreams', we have the general proposition, 'Whoever sleeps dreams' or 'If anyone sleeps, he dreams', written in the notation as 'For every value of x, if x sleeps, x dreams'; or its equivalent, 'No one sleeps without dreaming', which comes out as 'It is not the case that for some value of x, x sleeps and x does not dream.' (The two quantifiers, 'For some value of x' and 'For every value of x' are respectively called the existential and the universal quantifier.)

I need not elaborate on all the combinations and forms which these devices make possible. But there is one more device which I must mention. That is the sign of identity, with the aid of which we can express the fact, or the thought, that such-and-such a concept or combination of concepts has a unique application, applies in one and only one case; or again, in just two cases; and so on. Thus, for example, a doctrine of Christian theology concerning the unique joint application of the concepts of humanity and divinity could be expressed by the following formula: 'For some value of x ((*x* is human and *x* is divine) and (for every value of *y*, if *y* is human and *y* is divine, then *y* is identical with *x*))'; that is, 'Someone is both human and divine and is such that anyone both human and divine is identical with him.'

Here I end my very perfunctory sketch of the key notions of contemporary logic and its notation. The general logical notions involved are those of reference and predication, truth-functional composition, quantification, and identity. The notation in which the forms of proposition are represented consists correspondingly—if we abstract from all filling for the forms—of individual variables and predicate letters, propositional connectives, quantifiers, a sign of identity, and, of course, brackets or some other device to indicate the scope of connectives and quantifiers. This notation is called by Professor Quine 'canonical notation'. The name signalizes a claim— a claim of adequacy on behalf of the notation. The claim is that the notation reveals or embodies a clear and absolutely general framework which is adequate for all our propositional thinking, whatever its subject-matter.

We were to consider how such a revelation is to be connected with our ontological or metaphysical enquiry. If one took one sentence of Quine's out of context, it would seem that he, at least, regards the connection as remarkably close. He writes: 'The quest of a simplest, clearest overall pattern of canonical notation is not to be distinguished from a quest of ultimate categories, a limning of the most general traits of reality.'[2]

This remark, considered in itself, must surely be an exaggeration. A question about the basic concepts and categories in terms of which we organize our thinking about the world, our beliefs about how things are, must, it seems, be a question not only about the abstract framework of all thinking, but about the *filling* of that framework.

[2] Quine, *Word and Object* (New York, 1960), 161.

But it is worth following Quine further; for he soon enough shows that he too takes it that 'the quest for ultimate categories' is a matter of enquiring into how we fill, or how we should fill, the forms supplied by canonical notation. He has a quite explicit doctrine about our ontology—about what, at bottom, we take to exist. The doctrine gives a quite direct answer to the question of the relation between logic and ontology; and it demands our attention, both for its own sake and because it has, at least in the eyes of many, something of the character of the current orthodoxy. The doctrine is rather mysteriously stated, but its sense is not really obscure. What he says is that our ontology comprises just the things which the variables of quantification must range over, or take as values, if our beliefs are to be true. He even condenses his thought into an epigram: 'Tρ be is to be the value of a variable.' A memorable saying, but too concise to be readily understood.

However, we can approach the sense of the doctrine by a slightly indirect route. Suppose we are talking in all seriousness about the world, about reality as we conceive it. Suppose further that we employ a definite singular substantive with the intention of referring thereby to a particular individual object or person and attributing to it or him some property. Then what we say can be true, or even a candidate for truth, only on condition that such an object or person *exists* in fact. Again, if in the same spirit we attribute a property generally, without specifying a particular individual—i.e. if we say something of the form, 'For some x, x is such-and-such'—our assertion can be true only if there *exists* in fact some object or other which is such-and-such. If we are speaking in all seriousness, we must believe there are such items, or at least one such item. Equally, if we employ the universal quantifier, saying something of the form 'Every so-and-so is such-and-such'—or 'For every x, if x is so-and-so, then x is such-and-such'—then what we say cannot be true or, more precisely, cannot be true in a substantial and interesting fashion, unless there exist some things, or some thing, having the property signified by 'so-and-so'. (I put in the qualification about being 'true in an interesting fashion' since, given a truth-functional interpretation of 'if . . . then', what we say will be vacuously—hence uninterestingly—true if there are no such items.) In general, then, we believe in the existence of items of just those general kinds of which specimens must exist if these generalized predications, employing quantifiers are to be true (or, as in the last case, substantially and non-vacuously true). Here we have a paraphrase of the doctrine that our ontology comprises just sorts of things that our variables of quantification must range over if the general body of our beliefs is to be true. To put the point simply: if I say 'Someone smiles' or if I say 'Everyone who smiles is happy', the presumption is that I in each case believe in the existence of at least one smiling person; for, if there were no such person, what I say could not be true or at least, in the second case, could not be true except vacuously.

It should be noticed that Quine, in expounding his doctrine, speaks only of the range of values of the variables of quantification, whereas I began my explanation by speaking of reference, or intended reference, to determinate individuals by means of the use of definite singular substantives—something of which Quine makes no mention in stating his doctrine of ontological commitment. The reason is that he thinks that we can dispense with this way of directly designating individuals without loss, and that logical theory works more smoothly when definite singular terms are eliminated by paraphrase—as can always and easily be done, he maintains, by the use of the identity sign. That claim is controversial (in fact, I think, false), but the question is of no immediate importance. For it is obvious that you are equally committed to belief in the existence of something whether you name it directly or alternatively succeed in referring to it by employing a combination of predication, quantification, and the identity sign. In view of all this, we can perhaps simplify the statement of Quine's doctrine as follows: we are committed to belief in the existence of whatever kinds of thing we seriously refer to, or attempt to refer to, whether we refer generally, by way of variables of quantification, or determinately, by way of names or other definite singular terms. His supplementary doctrine, which accounts for his formulation of the ontological criterion, is that all references can be—and for logical clarity should be—carried by variables under quantification.

Now it is clear that we do not ordinarily express our beliefs in the notation of logic. So if we are to get the benefit of the promised insights into our ontological commitments, we should at least know in principle how to paraphrase our ordinary English sentences into canonical notation. And there seems to be no particular difficulty about this. Just as the logical language joins individual designations or variables under quantification to predicate expressions to form propositions, so ordinary English joins nouns or pronouns or noun phrases to predicate expressions to form propositions; and it is fairly easy to master the trick of rephrasing our sentences in such a way that these substantival expressions find themselves in the predicative position, while the referential or subject position is occupied by variables of quantification. For example, instead of, say, 'A woman has just telephoned', we write 'For some x, x is a woman and x has just telephoned'. Instead of 'All the workers are on strike', we write 'For every x, if x is a worker, x is on strike'. And here we see the variables of quantification ranging over, or having among their values, women in the first case, workers in the second; and learn, without surprise, that the serious speakers of these sentences are committed to belief in the existence of such items.

But now it will of course strike you that in our ordinary languages there is no restriction whatever on the general types or categories of items such that we can and do use nouns or noun phrases standing, or seeming to stand, for items belonging to those types or categories; and use them, moreover, in sentences in which, in all seriousness, we attach predicates to such expressions. Anything which can be mentioned at all can be mentioned by the use of some substantival locution. We have nouns or noun phrases not only for concrete individuals but also for times, places, quantities, properties, qualities, relations, propositions, numbers, facts, classes, species, events, actions, situations, states of mind, propositional attitudes, institutions, and so on and so on. So an indiscriminate and uncritical rewriting in canonical notation of all the sentences which we are disposed to accept as expressing truths would not seem likely to introduce any measure of selection or order into our ontology. We should simply find ourselves quantifying over items of all these types for which we have nouns or noun phrases. (The expression 'quantifying over' here is short for 'employing variables of quantification which must be assumed to range over'—in the sense already given to that expression.) So all I have just catalogued and more would find itself included without distinction in our ontology.

But of course it is not any such indiscriminate and uncritical style of paraphrase that Quine recommends as a guide to the nature of our basic ontology. What he recommends rather is a procedure of *critical* paraphrase, which is to be guided by two maxims. The first maxim requires that we employ only a vocabulary which is clear and scientifically acceptable; the second that we restrict our ontology to the minimum which would be theoretically sufficient for the expression of our beliefs, even if the price in practical convenience of observing such a restriction would be unacceptably high. The second maxim might be called the maxim of ontological economy. It may perhaps be seen simply as a consequence of the first in so far as Quine would regard only those of our beliefs which are themselves clear and scientifically acceptable as worthy of serious philosophical consideration. The apparent ontological excess which goes with the proliferation of nouns and noun phrases in our ordinary talk we can then charge to the account of mere practical convenience and brevity in discourse. We need not suppose we are seriously committed to belief in the actual existence of all the items such phrases may seem to stand for. We can, theoretically, express all that is scientifically acceptable in the beliefs for which we find it practically convenient to use such locutions by means of suitable paraphrase of those locutions; and since what we are seeking, or what Quine is seeking, is the fundametal ontology to which we are deeply committed by our fundamental and scientifically acceptable beliefs about reality, it is only those objects of reference which are from this point of view theoretically indispensable which are comprised in that ontology. Whence the maxim of ontological economy.

It is evident that we have here a programme of ontological reduction. I should like to compare it with that programme of reductive analysis of which I spoke earlier. There the drive was towards reduction of concepts by dismantling analysis or definition in terms of simpler concepts. Here the drive is towards reduction of commitment to entities (objects of reference) by means of critical paraphrase into canonical notation. But though their end results, if any, might be expected to be widely different, the second reductive drive has at least a certain formal resemblance to the first. Certain types of entity would appear as fundamental in the structure of our thought because the necessity of referring to them would survive the pressure of critical paraphrase. Others would disappear under this pressure. We are to explain them, indeed explain them away, by showing their dispensability and how they are dispensed with.

Now, I contrasted the reductive style of analysis with another kind—a kind which sought, not to reduce all concepts to a limited range of simpler elements, but rather to trace connections and establish, perhaps, priorities within a fundamental conceptual structure. Can we find a comparable contrast in the ontological field? The ontological reductionist draws, in principle, a single sharp distinction among the kinds of thing which, taking the loose and self-indulgent habits of our ordinary talk as our guide, we seem to refer to. There are those among them which we truly must regard as the indispensable objects of reference, those which resist the pressures of critical paraphrase; and there are the rest—the ones that can be pitched into the ontological dustbin. But one can easily imagine a less austere, a more tolerant and what might, in one sense, be called a more catholic, approach. Instead of just the saved and the lost, we might have an ontological hierarchy; instead of just the ins and the outs, an order of priority. For example, it might be agreed that attributes or properties are ontologically secondary to the objects to which one attributes them, in so far as reference to properties presupposes reference to objects, but not conversely. But agreement on this point would not require us either to deny the existence of properties or even to concede that we could, without seriously impoverishing our system of beliefs, dispense altogether with reference to, or quantification over, them. And in general we might find reason for saying that reference to items of certain types was secondary to, or derivative from, reference to items of other types without there being any implication that the former should therefore be, as it were, expelled from the domain of existence.

That suggestion would be quite consistent with another general proposal, already foreshadowed. The proposal is that, instead of asking: 'What are the objects of reference which survive the pressure

of critical paraphrase, conducted on severely Quinian principles?',
we should ask: 'What are the most general categories of things which
we *in fact* treat as objects of reference or—what comes to the same
thing—as subjects of predication and what are the most general
types of predicates or concepts which we employ *in fact* in speaking
of them?' Or, in other words: 'What are the fundamental types of
individuals, properties, and relations which characterize the structure
of our thought and what relations can be established among them?'
There is a set of ontological questions which are not without relation
to the fundamental notions of logic.

It might be objected that the above proposal suffers badly from
vagueness in comparison with Quine's definite and clear-cut
criterion of ontological commitment. No hint is given as to how we
should set about answering the recommended questions. There is
substance in this objection. We are, in fact, approaching the point at
which we must, so to speak, enrich the mixture of ontology and logic
by stirring in some epistemology as well. We shall not make any
progress until we do.

Nevertheless, before proceeding to do that, I should like first to
raise a more direct doubt about Quine's proposal. I raise it with
reference to a particular type of putative entity, viz. attributes or
properties, which Quine regards as ontologically inadmissible on the
grounds that, in contrast with classes, they lack a clear and general
criterion of identity. Let us suppose that we were satisfied that we
could, in principle, dispense with reference to or quantification over
properties, though not with reference to and quantification over
objects of the kinds of which the properties are predicated. Would it
really follow that our scheme of things was thereby shown to include
belief in the existence of the objects of the kinds in question but not
to include belief in the existence of the properties or attributes in
question? I shall give two quite different reasons that might be
advanced for doubting this consequence, and hence for questioning
the Quinian doctrine of ontological commitment.

The first reason that might occur to one is in fact very easily
disposed of if advanced as an objection to that doctrine. However, I
must mention it, since it is so obvious, even if only to get it out of the
way. It goes as follows. If we ordinarily say that we do not believe in

the existence of some attribute, say complete purity of heart or the property of being a natural slave, we should ordinarily and rightly be taken to mean that we do not believe that anyone can be truly said to be completely pure in heart or a natural slave; and the question whether this is so is of course something utterly different from the question of whether we need to refer to such attributes by means of a definite singular term or to regard them as falling within the range of values of our variables of quantification. Or again, when we say that, unlike the property of being a natural slave, poverty is something that does exist, we should ordinarily think it absurd to be told that we need hold no such belief if we are content to say instead that some people are poor. We should think it absurd because what we ordinarily mean by saying that poverty exists just is that some or many people are poor. So one of the things we ordinarily mean by saying of attributes or properties that they do or do not exist is something utterly different from what the doctrine in question would require us to mean.

However, as already suggested, this is not, as it stands, a very serious objection to the doctrine, i.e. to linking the notion of ontological commitment to that of indispensability as an object of reference. All that the objection requires by way of answer is that we recognize a secondary, though quite common, sense of 'exists'—a sense appropriate to properties and relations—in which to say that a certain property or relation exists is to say that there exist in the primary or fundamental sense of the word some things of which the property or relation in question can be truly predicated. The doctrine we are discussing, it may reasonably be said, is not a doctrine about the secondary sense at all, but only about the primary or fundamental sense of 'exists'. So once this distinction of senses is acknowledged, the point just made can also be acknowledged without any threat to the doctrine.

But this reply has no force at all against a second, also very simple, but different reason for questioning the doctrine. Suppose I say the following:

(A) There is at least one property which no machine possesses, viz. that of perfect efficiency.

Two things are quite clear. First, I can say this just as well by saying:

(B) No machine is perfectly efficient.

where, in (A) I quantify over properties, in (B) I do not. Second, whichever way I say it I am certainly not committed to the existence of the property of perfect efficiency in the common or secondary sense just discussed, i.e. to the view that something or other is perfectly efficient. On the contrary, I can perfectly consistently affirm that nothing whatever, let alone any machine, is perfectly efficient. If (A) carries a commitment to property existence, it will be in a quite different sense from that illustrated by the poverty example. So if there is any objection to saying that the paraphrasability of (A) by (B) shows that we need not be committed by (A) to belief in the existence of properties (or at least one property), then it will be quite a different objection from that which we have just considered and dismissed.

Is there any objection? Well, there is the extremely simple objection that (A) is a perfectly legitimate and correct way of saying what (B) says. If (B) is true, (A) is true, and true not merely in the secondary sense, but absolutely, in the primary sense. And if (A) is true absolutely, then there *is* at least one property which no machine possesses, i.e. there is at least one property. There *is* such a property and you really must admit there is, if you think (A) and (B) are true. It is no good saying that you don't have to say, in so many words, that there is such a property, since you can say (B) instead. You do not abolish your commitments by refusing to be explicit about them, any more than you can get rid of unpleasant realities by employing euphemisms.

I do not advance this very simple argument as a decisive objection to Quine's doctrine of ontological commitment. I am sure that adherents of that doctrine would dismiss it as readily as they would dismiss the first point, saying that it merely reflects an inessential feature of our language. But I mention it simply to suggest that the doctrine we have been discussing should be treated with a certain reserve. We can afford to treat it with reserve, since, as already indicated, we do not need to invoke this doctrine in order to raise some at least of the general metaphysical and ontological questions which we want to raise, and to raise them, moreover, in a form which makes clear their connection with basic logical notions.

Before we leave the doctrine, however, it is worth noting that it leaves us with a question: why is it found so natural, as Quine evidently finds it natural, to link the notion of existence so closely to that of indispensability as an object of reference or subject of predication? There is surely something that needs explaining here. I note now the fact that it does for subsequent reference.

❖ 4 ❖

Logic, Epistemology, Ontology

So far I have made little mention of the third member of our philosophical trio: ontology, logic, epistemology. The moment has come, as I suggested a little earlier, at which, in order to make progress, we must invoke this third member, the theory of knowledge, and bring it into relation with its two partners.

Let us first recall the way in which logic came into the picture. The use of concepts, I said, following Kant, or their fundamental use, is in judgement, the conscious forming or holding of beliefs about what is the case. Hence the relevance of that study which concerns itself with the general forms of judgement and their relations. Now the aim of judgement is truth. We want, with good reason, to form true beliefs rather than false beliefs; and a given judgement or belief is true just in so far as things are in fact as one who makes that judgement or holds that belief thereby believes them to be. This is the platitude enshrined in anything which calls itself a Correspondence Theory of Truth. Mistakes have been made in the name of that theory, as we shall see. But one of the merits of the name—'correspondence'—is that it brings out the point that over against judgement and belief is the natural world or reality, the things and events to which our judgements or beliefs relate or which they are *about*; and that it is how things are in the natural world, in reality or in fact, that determines whether our judgements or beliefs are true or false.

Or, at least, this seems to be correct for a very fundamental and important class of our judgements or beliefs. Perhaps not—or not so straightforwardly—for all. We speak, for instance, of moral judgements as true or false; but it is a matter of debate just how moral judgements are related to natural facts. Or again, we speak of truths of logic and of pure mathematics; and it can be held that these are regions in which thought, as it were, feeds on itself to generate structures which are quite independent, as regards their validity, of the way things are in reality. This view can be held. It can also be denied in the name of a distinctive mathematical reality; or it can be rejected as resting on an untenable distinction regarding the ways in which beliefs are validated. But at any rate there is matter for debate here also.

For the time being we may leave these debates aside; for the judgements, the propositions, we are most fundamentally concerned with certainly are judgements about how things are in the natural world; and how they indeed are is what determines these judgements as true or false. So we have, on the one hand, the use of concepts in judgement or belief; on the other, the reality, the world, the facts; and the state of the latter determines the truth or falsity of the former.

The picture I am presenting here has a certain deliberate crudity. I present it like this in order to force a certain question and a certain answer to the question. The question is: how does the concept-user come to *form* beliefs about the reality. And the natural answer is: he is made *aware* of the reality in *experience*; experience of the world enables him to use concepts in judgement about it.

The question and the reply could both be said to be of an epistemological order. But the picture is still too simple. It is not that experience is, as it were, simply a convenient link with the world; enabling the concept-user to go into action as a judgement-former with a fair prospect of forming true beliefs. The connection between judgement, concept, and experience is closer than that. The connection is, rather, that concepts of the real can mean nothing to the user of them except in so far as they relate, directly or indirectly, to possible experience of the real. It is not just that without experience of the real we should not be able to form true beliefs about it; it is that the very concepts in terms of which we form our primitive or fundamental or least theoretical beliefs get their sense for us precisely *as* concepts which we should judge to apply in possible experience situations.

I am putting this point too very crudely and roughly. It will have to be refined. But what I am putting thus crudely and roughly is the central tenet of *empiricism*. It is the truth on which Kant insisted decisively, and on which all empiricists before and since have also insisted. The reason why Kant's insistence was the decisive one was that he went a long way to free this principle from certain confusions which were inherent in earlier and some later empiricists' understanding of it. He freed the principle from the errors of classical or atomistic empiricism.

It should be added, however, that there is one particular basic risk associated with this important principle, a risk which it is not clear that Kant himself entirely avoided. I said that the dualistic picture I began with—the picture of the concept-user forming judgements on the one hand and, on the other, the reality about which he judges and which determines the truth or falsity of his judgements—that this picture was too simple, and that it remained too simple when a reference to experience was added as what made such judgement possible. The picture needed supplementing with the empiricist insistence that concepts have no role in knowledge, are empty, as Kant puts it, except in relation to possible experience. Let us call the initial duality here 'the duality of the judging Subject and the Objective Reality about which he judges'. The risk I am now speaking of, the risk inherent in the empiricist insistence, is the risk of losing hold of this duality altogether. In insisting that experience not only bridges the gap between Subject and Object, but also gives the concepts we use all their sense of content, we run the risk of the notion of objective reality being entirely engulfed or swallowed up in that of experience. Many idealisms and all phenomenalisms are the results of this engulfing; and the history of much of our epistemology, when it isn't one of sinking into (or wallowing in) this gulf, is one of struggle to get out of it, to show that various forms of scepticism about the Objective Reality are unwarranted. But it is better to avoid the gulf altogether.

So far we have avoided it indeed; so let us see if we can develop our theme while continuing to avoid it.

And now back to logic for a moment: to the fundamental form of uncompounded judgement and to the fundamental functions which characterize it; that is, to the combination of reference and predication. Our task is to connect this logical notion with two others: on the one hand with the ontological notion of the objective reality about which we judge; on the other hand with the epistemological notion of experience which alone gives sense and content to our judgements. The fundamental form of affirmative judgement, then, is that in which we judge that some *general* concept has application in some *particular* case. You will see that this description is really ambiguous as between two types of form: the forms of *atomic* propositions in the verbal expression of which no quantifiers occur and the particular case is specified by naming or otherwise designating the particular individual or individuals to which the concept is applied; and the existentially quantified form in which the general concept is judged to have application in some particular unspecified case or other. (For example: 'John is singing' and 'Someone is singing'.) We can rest with this ambiguity as untroublesome and even possibly useful. For what we have to ask is a very general question: what are we to understand, in connection with the notion of making a judgement about an objective reality, by the notion of *a particular case* in which a *general concept* applies?

Well, a general concept is general in this sense: it is capable, in principle, of being exemplified in any number of different particular cases. Our grasp of a concept must include our grasp of this possibility. But, as we have just seen, our grasp of a concept of the objectively real cannot be separated from the notion of a possible application of that concept in experience. So it must be possible in principle for us—if we are to have any use of concepts at all—*to encounter in experience different particular cases and distinguish them as different while also recognizing them as alike in being all cases apt for the application of the same concept.* Now what is the foundation, the underlying ground, of this possibility?

Here is the point at which it is necessary to introduce, and to connect with the notion of different particular instances of the same concept, the two great notions of Space and Time. Evidently our experience is temporal, successive, stretching before and after;

evidently also our experience is such as to offer us, at any moment, a spatial extent or volume, extending from a centre, the centre, we might say, of our personal experience. Correspondingly, our picture of objective reality is a picture of a world in which things are separated and related in time and space; in which different particular objects coexist and have histories; in which different events happen successively and simultaneously; in which different processes complete themselves over time. Obviously these notions need examination if we are to show how they all fit together in our scheme of things. My immediate purpose is simply to connect the notions of spatiality and temporality (Space and Time) with that of different particular cases or instances of a general concept; that is, with the logical notion of an individual object.

And see how easily this connection is made. Surveying a spatial extent, we may distinguish, at the same moment, different particular instances of one general concept, as when we see at once two sheep in a field or two red triangles on a screen. Here spatial, not temporal, separation and relation are invoked. But we can as easily invoke the other dimension, where temporal, not spatial separation is involved: the series of successive instances of the same sound as the clock strikes twelve. Or we can mix both cases together.

One can imagine an objection in the form of a question. Why thus accord a special role to the notions of space and time in seeking an empirical foundation for the idea of different particular instances of a general concept, hence for the very idea of the generality of a concept? Is it not the case that different particular instances of a general concept will normally be distinguished by something else than the difference of spatial or temporal position? My car is indeed in a different spatial position from your car; but that is not the only difference between them; my car has a scratch and yours has not. Was it not Leibniz who insisted that every leaf in the forest could be seen to differ from every other if you looked hard enough for the difference? And even if it is not always so, is it not enough that it could always be so?

The answer to this objection is very simple. Suppose it to be the case that every two leaves differ from each other in some respect other than the spatio-temporal. The fact remains that you would not, and could not, have *two* leaves thus to differ further, *unless* they differed spatio-temporally. It is impossible that there should be two leaves which differed from each other in some other respect but which were spatio-temporally indistinguishable.

It might now be said: this simple answer is a question-begging one. It may be true of concepts of spatio-temporal things that if two instances of one such concept differ at all, i.e. if they are two, then they differ spatio-temporally. But might there not be general concepts of the objectively real—concepts of individual objects in reality—which were not concepts of spatio-temporal things at all?

But the reply to this question is equally evident, once we remember that we are looking for an empirical foundation, a foundation *in experience*, for the idea in question. The reply consists in evoking the empiricist principle. The condition of our having general concepts of the objectively real, of objects in nature, which were not concepts of spatio-temporal things at all would be our enjoyment of a certain kind of experience—an experience in which space and time either played no part at all or at least were totally unrelated to our wholly empirical awareness of the numerical difference of different particular instances of one and the same such concept. It is here that the empiricist principle exerts its power. For this supposed description of a kind of experience remains for us quite empty, a mere form of words, without empirical significance; and the notion of general concepts of empirical objects which were not concepts of the spatial or the temporal remains equally empty. (It will be seen that I here echo Kant's doctrine of the forms of sensibility.)

The objector has a last resource. Let it be admitted, he says, that the notion of a possible experience of a plurality of different cases of one and the same concept has an essential relation either to the feature of spatiality or to that of temporality—either to spatial or to temporal separation and relatedness. Yet why insist on both? Would not temporality by itself suffice? Or spatiality by itself? We have indeed, in fact, experience (communion with Nature, one might say) in both kinds. But can we not, for this very reason, understand very well the possibility of the requirements of judgements of the real being satisfied by communion in one kind only? Can we not understand the thought of judgement about the real being based on experience of it which was temporal but not spatial? Or even spatial but not temporal? In entertaining this thought, we are surely not going beyond possible experience in the way forbidden by the empiricist principle. We are simply imagining experience more limited than it actually is.

It is possible to argue against this thought. It is possible to argue against it on the grounds that it takes us not beyond the upper limits but beyond what I earlier called the lower limits of sense; not on the ground that it introduces empty notions, but on the ground that it tries to discard essential notions; not because it adds to our working model purely non-functional pieces which have no work to do, but because it leaves us with too few pieces for the model to work at all. I have referred to this type of argument earlier, in discussing, with reference to Kant, a very strong sense of 'basic' in which it might be claimed that certain features of our conceptual scheme were basic, i.e. essential to any truly coherent conception of experience that we could form. But I shall not try to argue this now. For our immediate purpose is the more modest one of trying to sketch the basic general features of the conceptual structure we actually have, and the relations between them, without enquiring which of these features are also basic in this very strong sense; and on these terms we may readily agree that the connection of the notions of *both* space and time with the notion of different particular instances of a general concept is indeed a basic general feature of our conceptual structure.

Parenthetically I may perhaps venture here on a partial explanation of something which I earlier said needed explaining. I refer to Quine's thesis regarding ontological commitment and the associated drive for ontological economy. I have just been discussing some fundamental cases of judgement about the objectively real— judgements to the effect that some general concept has application in some particular case. And in the case of such judgements I have just established a connection between two distinctions: on the one hand, the logical distinction between reference and predication; on the other hand, the ontological distinction between spatio-temporal individuals (which I shall henceforth call 'particulars' simply) and the general concepts of property or relation of which the particulars provide examples. For I have argued that it is precisely

these spatio-temporal objects, the particulars, that are the fundamental objects of reference or subjects of predication. If this is so,
perhaps we have a clue to the doctrine that we are really committed
to belief in the existence of just those things which we absolutely
must treat as objects of reference if we are to be able to express our
beliefs (or, at least, those of our beliefs which pass the test of
scientific acceptability). It is clearly true that we must treat as objects
of reference those things which are the fundamental objects of
reference in all discourse about objective reality, i.e. the particulars.
Suppose now that the notion of existence was already linked in our
minds with the notion of individual particulars—things of which the
very identity is bound up with the spatio-temporal distinguishability
of each one from others of its kind. Suppose, that is, that we are
naturally predisposed to think of the individual particular, with a
place of its own in space and time, as the very paradigm or model of
the genuinely existent, the real. (It is no falsification of our natural
prejudices to suppose this.) Now add to this the fact I have just
stressed—that in our basic judgements about objective reality it
seems that spatio-temporal individuals will in fact be the objects of
reference or, as Quine would say, the items over which our variables
of quantification range. If we take these two points together, we
perhaps have at least part of the explanation we earlier noticed the
need of: that is, the explanation both of the view that what we really
believe in the existence of is what we cannot but treat as objects of
reference, and of the associated drive towards ontological economy,
the desire to keep these ontological commitments to a minimum.

To say that we have a partial explanation of that drive is not to say
that we have a justification for it. On the contrary. For if it is indeed
an explanation, then it may seem that the drive towards ontological
reduction may be in part attributable to an unwarranted fear: the
fear that the admission to one's ontology of certain abstract or non-
particular things (such as properties, propositions, etc.) involves the
risk of myth-making, of treating such things as more like particular
spatio-temporal objects than they are. (Think of the common
philosophical talk of overpopulating the universe etc.) The danger
may be real; but it seems to me that it can be avoided without
yielding to the reductive pressure.

✦⇝ 5 ⇜✦

Sensible Experience and Material Objects

NOW it is time to develop, to fill out a little, the notion of the concept-using subject's *experience* of the objective world, and of that experience yielding true judgements about the world. Here so many considerations came together at once that it is difficult to keep a grasp of them all at once, let alone order them in a clear way. Something we might try holding on to at first is suggested by the two words 'here' and 'now'. The concept-user's awareness of the world is awareness *from* a certain spatial point of view *at* any moment. His awareness, of course, is constantly changing, though perhaps only in small ways, either because the world changes within the range of his awareness of it or because his orientation towards it, his spatial point of view on it, changes, or because of both at once. Just as 'here' implies an awareness of the world as extending in space away from the subject's point of view on it, so 'now' implies a sense of the past and of the subject's awareness of it (memory) and a sense of its possible or probable future (expectation). The point which, above all, we must retain a secure grip of—apparently not an easy thing to do—is the point that the subject's experience of the world is conceived of both as something *in* the world, a part of the world and its history, and also genuinely an experience *of* the world and hence the source of objective judgements about it. The words 'here' and 'now' help us to do this because of their evident double reference: together they indicate, as it were, a particular reference point in an objective spatio-temporal world; but it is only relative to particular *subjects* at particular times that they have that *objective* reference. One cannot, as it were, detach 'here' and 'now' from all occasions of occurrence in the mouths or minds of experiencing subjects and still meaningfully ask what space–time point or region in the objective world they refer to. The question would be emptied of sense.

So then, we have the notion of the concept-user's temporally extended experience from a point of view—an experience which is both *in* and *of* a spatio-temporally objective world. Now this notion is precisely the most general form of the notion of *sense perception*—a topic which might be said to have been, not long ago, almost a professional obsession of British empiricist philosophers.

So what is involved in the notion of sense perception yielding true judgements about an objective spatio-temporal world? Of course, in asking this question, it is not implied that sense perception always yields true judgements. We can, and do, misperceive, make mistakes. But it is certainly a feature of our ordinary scheme of thought that sense perception is taken to yield judgements which are generally or usually true. Remember that in thinking of the world as objective, we are thinking of it as being the way it is independently of any particular judgement about it; the truth of the judgement, if it *is* true, consists in its conformity to the way things are in the world. Hence the minimum that seems to be involved in the notion of sense perception generally yielding true judgements about an objective spatio-temporal world is that there should be some pretty regular relation of dependence of the experience enjoyed in sense perception on the way things objectively are. (Otherwise the normal truth or correctness of perceptual judgements would seem to be something inexplicable, an extraordinary coincidence.)

Evidently this quite general notion of dependence must be qualified to take account of the fact that the range of experience of any subject at any time is limited; so that experience at any moment will depend only on certain parts or aspects of the objective world.

We have, then, this notion of experience occurring in time and having a certain character which is dependent on a certain spatio-temporal distribution of objective features in relation to a certain central spatial region, the region occupied by the subject; and this is, in the broadest sense, a notion of the *causal dependence* of the experience on the objective features in question. And the point I want to make now is that this notion of the causal dependence of the experience enjoyed in sense-perception on features of the objective spatio-temporal world is implicit from the very start in the notion of sense perception, given that the latter is thought of as generally issuing in true judgements about the world. It is not something we discover with the advance of science, or even by refined common observation. Neither does it require any refined philosophical argument. It is conceptually inherent in a gross and obvious way in the very notion of sense perception as yielding true judgements about an objective spatio-temporal world. Hence any philosophical theory which seeks to be faithful to our general framework of ideas, our general system of thought, must provide for this general notion of causal dependence. It must, to this extent at least, be a causal theory of perception. Of course, what we do find out by refined or scientific observation and investigation is how this general relation of causal dependence is actually realized, what forms it takes, what mechanisms are involved in it. These questions also have their philosophical interest—as we shall see.

For the moment I leave those questions on one side, in order to examine more carefully the conception we have arrived at. The idea we now have is that of any slice of experience being somehow centred in some spatio-temporal region of the world and being dependent for its character and occurrence on a certain distribution of objective features in the regions surrounding this centre. But clearly more than this centring and this causal dependence is involved. For a thing to have experience, it is not sufficient that it should be located in space and time and respond systematically to its environment. So much could be said of a plant or an instrument. But we are speaking of something which is not merely sensitive to its environment, as a plant or an instrument might be, but of which the sensitivity takes the form of conscious awareness of its environment. We are speaking of subjects who employ concepts in forming judgements about the world—judgements which issue from the experience enjoyed in sense perception.

Now the way in which I have just expressed myself—the phrase I have just used—can be misleading. It may tempt us to picture to ourselves two distinct stages in the formation of perceptual judgements, in the following way: first (Stage 1) there is sensible experience, sensation in various modes, the outcome of the influence of the environment on the senses; and then, second (Stage 2) there is judgement, the deploying of concepts in the formation of beliefs about the world on the basis of this sensible experience. And there are in fact philosophers who do adopt this picture of two causal stages: of sensible experience being caused by the environment and in its turn causing judgement, the forming of belief. So, according to this picture, sensible experience would be something, no doubt rich and complex enough, but not much attended to except for special purposes—clinical or aesthetic—since its main function would be that of acting as the immediate causal agent in the promotion of beliefs about the world, the causing of judgement.

I think this is the wrong image. It is wrong because the concepts employed in perceptual judgement about the world, on the one hand, and sensible experience itself, on the other, interpenetrate each other more closely than this picture suggests. I have remarked on the general empiricist principle that concepts are empty, have no significance for us, unless we can relate them, directly or indirectly, to experience, to experiential conditions for their application. Of course the relation of concepts to experience must be particularly close in the case of those ordinary, commonplace, pre-theoretical concepts in terms of which we formulate our naïve perceptual judgements. And the closeness of this relation is not (cannot be) a one-sided affair. Just as concepts, or at least these relatively commonplace concepts, get their sense in and from perceptual experience, so perceptual experience gets its character from the concepts we deploy in our naïve perceptual judgements. The character of our perceptual experience itself, of our sense experience itself, is thoroughly conditioned by the judgements about the objective world which we are disposed to make when we have this experience; it is, so to speak, thoroughly permeated—saturated, one might say—with the concepts employed in such judgements. That is to say, the candid description of experience at any moment must normally be given in terms of those concepts; and not in the restricted terms which are appropriate at moments when the subject's attention is engaged only by sensations of special, e.g. clinical or aesthetic, interest.

For example, the best way, indeed normally the only way, of giving a veridical description of your current visual experience—of the visual experience which you, my reader, are having at the moment—is to describe what you take yourselves to be *seeing* out there is the world in front of you. You can always take precautions against the remote possibility of error by employing a formula such as 'My visual experience is as of seeing . . .' and then carrying on with the description in the same terms as before. The point is that the concepts which are necessary for the experience description are precisely those which are necessary for the world description. Similarly, as regards your current auditory experience, your present sensible experience is of (or as of) hearing these words being pronounced in such and such a tone of voice.[1] Of course there are sometimes occasions on which there is good reason to hedge, or qualify, our judgement; but then too we use the same concepts as if we were judging without reserve, but add an explicit indication of reserve: such as, for example, 'It looks as if such-and-such; but it may be an illusion'.

It is time to take another step forward—or, perhaps better, to examine another link. We were to develop or fill out the common notion of sense perception yielding true judgements about an objective spatio-temporal world. So far I have remarked that perceptual experience must be causally sensitive to the externally environing world, and also that it is thoroughly penetrated by the concepts we employ in forming perceptual judgements about that world. But it is also clear that if those judgements are to be in general true, then the concepts employed in those judgements must in general be concepts of kinds of things which actually are in the world and of properties which those things actually have.

In saying this, I am not posing, nor am I solving, a sceptical problem. I have not produced a proof of anything. But neither am I going on to ask what guarantee we can have that this is actually so. What would it be to ask this? Well, it might be one of two things. It

---

[1] The terms of this sentence reflect its source—in lectures given by the author.

might be an invitation to step outside the entire structure of the conceptual scheme which we actually have—and then to justify it from some extraneous point of vantage. But there is nowhere to step; there is no such extraneous point of vantage. Evidently, then, the search for such a guarantee must be understood differently. What we are invited to do, rather, is to take a stand on what seems to be some peculiarly secure part of the structure, and then to justify or reinterpret or reconstruct the rest of it, or the problematic parts, from this secure base. This is the procedure of several philosophies, including, above all, classical empiricism in its various forms; all of which forms, as I shall attempt to show later, end in distortion and failure.

So, then, I am neither posing a problem nor proposing a solution. I am simply tracing the lines which connect with each other the parts of the structure. This is not to say that the structure can never be modified. It can be modified from within itself by the advance of knowledge gained from within. I do not mean merely that we gain more knowledge of the world, though of course we do this. I mean rather that our very conception of the basic structure of ideas within which this gain in knowledge is made can be refined as a result of such gains. The point which we have now reached is a point at which this fact can be illustrated—by reference to a famous philosophical crux, which I shall now approach.

Our sensible experience is permeated, we say, by concepts of the objective world, the world spread out in space and time, how things are in which determines the truth or falsity of our judgements. Concentrating for a moment on the spatial aspect of the matter, we see that consequently our concepts of the objective will include what in the most general possible terms we might call concepts of modes of *occupancy* of space. Of course we will have concepts of spatial relation—of relative position in space—but also we will have concepts of spatial properties characterizing the occupants of positions in space—concepts, that is, of shape and size (or, as John Locke puts it, of figure and bulk). So our concepts of the objective world will be above all concepts of things which have both spatial properties and spatial positions. And it is obvious that this condition is in fact met by many ordinary concepts of the objective which enter into our perceptual judgements, such as all our concepts of animals, plants, artefacts, geographical features, etc.

But there is more to be said. The notions of spatial position, extent, shape, and size are relatively abstract notions; for, as Berkeley insisted, we cannot become perceptually aware of the position, extent, and shape of some occupant of space except by becoming aware of these spatial properties in some specific sensible or sensory mode. The spatial properties or relations must be discriminated by us by way of the specific properties of the sensory modality in question. Thus we become aware of the shape, size, and position of occupants of space by way of awareness of boundaries defined by visual and tactile qualities, in subtle relation to each other and to other types of sensible experience: we become aware of objects in space *as* coloured or shaded in various ways or as hard, smooth, soft, rough, yielding, or resistant. The relevant range of concepts of essentially visual or tactile qualities is as intimately associated with those concepts of spatial objects which enter into our perceptual judgements as are the more abstract spatial concepts. If I say I have bought a horse, you may just as appropriately ask *what colour* it is as *where* it is stabled or *how high* it stands.

And now to the problem. When we learn something of the causal mechanisms of perception—of the physics and physiology of perception—our whole view of the matter may undergo a certain radical shift or displacement. There are writers, particularly those who write on the physiology of perception, who regularly describe as 'purely subjective' those sensible qualities which are peculiar to one sensible modality—including therefore visual and tactile qualities, colour and felt texture. They mean that the fact that we perceive things as having those sensible qualities is a causal consequence both of the physical constitution of the things themselves and of our own physiological make-up. Had our make-up been different, we would have perceived things differently. The conclusion that seems to be implied by the use of the word 'subjective'—a conclusion that is sometimes explicitly drawn—is that no such sensible qualities as we normally understand them really or intrinsically belong to the things that occupy space; these things really possess only the physical properties which are ascribed to them in the physical theories in terms of which the physico-physiological mechanisms of perception are explained. But these physical properties, though involving spatial position and spatial configurations, are, in the sense already explained, abstract: their specification includes no reference to the qualities peculiar to any sensory modality in which we might become aware of them. So we have the consequence that, though we can, in a sense, perceive objects in space, we cannot perceive them *as they really are*, or as they are in themselves, at all. And this is not a situation that could be remedied by any modification of our perceptual equipment or by the help of any instruments, however refined; for, whatever modifications were introduced or instruments used, perception would always be mediated by sensible qualities of some kind. So things can be conceived, thought of, in abstract terms, as they really are; but they cannot become objects of perception as they really are. We do perceive things indeed, but not as they really are, only as they appear to beings physiologically constituted as we are.

The thing to appreciate about this conclusion is that, properly understood, it is both perfectly acceptable and, at the same time, perfectly compatible with the proposition that we normally do perceive things as they really are. The two propositions, though in appearance each other's contradictories, are not really so, because the phrase 'things as they really are' is used with different senses, or different criteria of application, in the two propositions. In the sense in which it is used in the first proposition, all ascription to things of qualities peculiar to a given sensory mode—as colour, felt texture, etc.—is excluded from the description of things as they really are; the standard of reality is physical theory. In the more ordinary sense in which the phrase is used in the second proposition, such ascription is not excluded; it is those ascriptions (of sensible qualities) which are associated with normal conditions of observation that are taken as the standard by which others are corrected. Provided that we distinguish the two uses of 'real' or 'reality', we can grant to each standpoint, each standard, its own validity. From both standpoints alike, we are speaking of the same things; for identity of reference to those things is secured by the fact that ascription of the gross spatial characteristics of position, size, and shape—of occupation, in a word, of a certain region of space—is something common to both styles of description.

I put forward this familiar philosophical crux as an example of the way in which our view of our own basic structure of ideas can be shifted or modified as a result of developments from within it; and in order to show, at the same time, how philosophy can help us to keep our balance when such shifts occur.

One can easily imagine an objection. Someone might say: 'You haven't really drawn the sting of the scientific argument. You say that certain ascriptions of sensible qualities are accepted as a standard by which other such ascriptions are corrected. But all that is purely human and subjective; it has nothing to do with the physical facts, which are what they are quite independently of subjective human sensibility.' Now here, I think, we have a typically obsessive reaction. We should note, first, what has happened to the word 'subjective': it has lost its contrast with 'intersubjective', which standard ascriptions of sensible qualities typically are. Obsessed with a particular, scientific aspect of our concern with the objective world, the objector has associated the notion of objectivity exclusively with that concern, and so has lost altogether the sense of the part which concepts of the objective play in our lives as acting, social, and intercommunicating beings. What he has perhaps more fundamentally lost sight of is the fact that objects must be perceived as bearers of sensible qualities, visual and tactile, if they are to be perceived as space-occupiers at all. And this is why the ascription to them of sensible qualities, the standard of correctness of such ascription being intersubjective agreement, is something quite securely rooted in our conceptual scheme.

To return to the starting-point of this last discussion. I there insisted above all on the spatial dimension of our conception of the objective world. Obviously there is also the dimension of time to be considered. I earlier emphasized that the subject's experience of the objective world is experience *from* a certain spatial point of view *at* some moment and that this is necessarily how he himself conceives of it. The little phrase 'here and now', I said, reverberates with this thought. The subject could not attach any sense to this phrase unless he had the conception of an objective spatio-temporal world from within which he has experience of it; and equally he could not have that conception unless he had mastered the notions those words express. But this conception involves more than I have so far explicitly said. And we can begin to understand what more it involves by reference to the notion of change of the perceiver's point of view relative to objects perceived.

Evidently—and this would be true if we were thinking, not specifically of change of the perceiver's point of view relative to objects perceived, but of change of any kind in his experience of the world—we need the idea of some retention of the content of judgements made at earlier points in the process of change. We need, at least, some form of memory on the part of the judging subject—some sense of the past (and of the future)—to give force to 'now'. But, and this is the point I want to stress, we need more than this. In order for the very notion of a spatial point of view on an objective world to have empirical or experiential content, hence to have any sense, it is necessary for the subject to be able to have, and to make empirical application of, the notion of the persisting identity of at least some of the objects which fall within the scope of his changing perceptions. The changes in his point of view must be, and must be experienced as, relative to objects which persist through those changes. Moreover, it is clear that this notion of retention of identity on the part of objects perceived must be embodied in at least some of the concepts which enter into the subject's judgements of perception; that is to say, in the ordinary concepts of objects which, as previously remarked, are indispensable to a veridical account of our sensible experience. Hence, we perceive some or much of what we perceive *as* relatively enduring space-occupying entities, entities of such sorts that they retain their identities when we perceive different aspects of them from different points of view or when, as a result of one kind of change or another, they cease to be within our immediate perceptual range. Over time each of us builds up a detailed picture of the world. But all the detailed pictures, built up over time by different subjects of experience, have a common basic structure: they are all pictures of a world in which each of us occupies, at any moment, some perceptual point of view; and in which space-occupying individuals, distinguished or distinguishable as such under concepts of such things, have, as we have, past histories, and, perhaps, a future.

So these identity-retaining, space-occupying individuals—which, in our experience, are, in general, what we may call 'material objects' or 'bodies'—occupy a quite fundamental position in our scheme of things, in the conceptual structure we employ. A conclusion which I foreshadowed a good while previously. These objects, with their changes, their relations, and their interactions, constitute, or yield, the unitary spatio-temporal framework of our world.

The fact is reflected in our language, as we might expect it to be. These identity-preserving, space-occupying individuals—material objects and, or including, people—are the primary referents of our nouns and noun phrases. Of course, as I emphasized in my discussion of Quine's doctrine of ontological commitment, we have, and employ, nouns and noun phrases for a huge variety of other kinds of thing—indeed for things of any type of category you like to name. But these other nouns and noun phrases are, in general, grammatically derivative: they derive from adjectives or adjectival phrases, from verbs or verb phrases, or from complete clauses; or, alternatively, they are modelled on nouns or noun phrases so derived. It can be seen how this point connects with the notion of ontological ordering which I earlier sketched. Language offers us a reflection of the fundamental place, in our scheme of things, of certain types of objects of reference, of logical individuals; and hence also of the primacy of certain types of predication, of types of properties and relations.

✦❧ 6 ❧✦

Classical Empiricism.
The Inner and the Outer
Action and Society

S o far my project has been that of tracing some of the principal lines
of connection and interdependence which link together the fundamental concepts of our general structure of ideas. I need hardly say
that this project is far from completion. But now I want to interrupt
its progress for a while in order to set it in contrast with a quite
different approach, or family of approaches, to this general structure
of ideas; a family of approaches to which I have already alluded, and
which, indeed, until relatively recently, dominated the British
empiricist tradition in philosophy. It is with the intention of
bringing out more clearly the character of my own approach that I
undertake the task of characterizing this opposed, and in my view
mistaken, tradition.

According to this tradition, as I have already remarked, the
general structure of our ideas is to be seen as derived, in one way or
another, from a certain small part of itself. This fundamental part of
the structure is conceived as basic and underived; as *given*. It
consists in the temporally ordered sequence of subjective mental
states, including above all sensory experiences, in the mind of the
subject; and, in accordance with that over-sharp separation of
sensible experience and judgement which I referred to earlier, these
mental states themselves are often rather narrowly conceived as
impressions or images of simple sensory qualities, alone or in

combination. These, and these alone, are the basic materials. In relation to this basis the rest of the ordinary structure of our thinking is conceived of in various ways, depending on which variety of this kind of empiricism is in question. For there are three principal varieties, which I shall now try to distinguish.

According to one of them, the general structure of our thought, of our ordinary beliefs about the world, is to be regarded as a kind of *theory*, elaborated on the basis of the sequence of subjective states; and hence calling for *rational justification* in somewhat the way in which what we more ordinarily regard as scientific theories about the world or reality call for rational justification. According to a second variety of the approach, the general structure of our beliefs is thought of, not as a theory which calls for a reasoned justification, but rather as a way of thinking to which we are naturally committed, which we cannot help accepting or—to put it crudely—which we are stuck with; but the fact that we are thus naturally committed to such a way of thinking calls, on this view, for a natural, i.e. a scientific, explanation—an explanation to be framed, of course, in terms only of the basic materials. This is David Hume's variety of the empiricist approach; as, most evidently, when he says that it is useless to enquire whether there are bodies or not, since we cannot help believing that there are; the proper question to ask is what causes us to believe in their existence. Hume's own reply to this question is, of course, as already remarked, given in terms of the basic subjective states and of psychological laws which can be formulated in terms of them; nothing else is to be allowed in the explanation. There is yet a third type of empiricist theory, according to which all the notions which constitute the general structure of our thought, apart from the elements admitted as basic, are what used to be called 'logical constructions' out of those basic elements; that is to say, all other notions, if admissible at all, could in principle be defined in terms of the basic elements and of such relations as those elements were intrinsically capable of. Ontologically speaking, on this version, the only items of which we are really obliged to admit the existence are these basic elements, the subjective states, themselves. Certainly we are entitled to speak freely, as we do, of the existence of other types of things—of bodies, intersubjective space, other subjects of experience, etc.; but all such talk is only a convenient, indeed practically indispensable, way of abbreviating propositions which could in principle be reduced to the basic elements. It is evident that, of the three types of empiricist approach I have distinguished, it is this third, essentially reductive, variety which comes closest to that conceptual atomism of which I spoke earlier.

I have drawn sharp divisions between the three varieties; but elements of different varieties may sometimes be mixed together to produce a composite variety belonging to the same family. Or one may find a philosopher of this general persuasion giving up one of these three approaches in favour of another of the same family. For example, Professor Ayer, once an adherent of the third, later preferred a theory in which the first is mingled with the second. Perhaps the most daring and, as one might say, breath-taking of these approaches is the second, that of Hume; in its pure form, it is, I think, peculiar to him among the notable philosophers of this general persuasion. But any philosopher of this school will think that one or another of these approaches—or some composite variant of them—must be right, that they are exhaustive of the possibilities. And this view—that they are exhaustive alternatives—might be said to be the defining characteristic of *classical empiricism*. What I here call classical empiricism must not be confused with what I earlier described as the central principle of empiricism in general, a principle which should continue to command our respect and on which Kant, as I said, insisted in a fashion which was decisive, precisely because he freed the principle from the confusions and limitations of classical empiricism. One may think that Kant, while avoiding these limitations, encased his correct understanding of the principle in a doctrine—that of transcendental idealism—which violated it; but even if so, it may still be possible to detach what is valid in his interpretation from the casing which surrounds it; whereas the confusions and limitations of classical empiricism are inherent in it.

I hope it is now clear how the path I have been following stands in contrast with the path, or paths, followed by the classical empiricists. I take each variety of their approach in turn. First, there is, on my view, no question of justifying the general structure of ideas within which I have been tracing some of the principal connections—no question of justifying it on the narrow basis of that part of it which consists in the notion of a temporally ordered sequence of subjective states. On the contrary. It is the general structure of ideas itself, the general framework of our thought, which is the basic thing, the foundation of our intellectual economy. Every rational justification of theory about reality presupposes and rests upon this general structure. Second, as for explanation: a natural explanation, such as Hume endeavoured to give on the narrow empiricist basis, of the development in the growing individual of the mastery of this framework of notions—an explanation of the ontogenesis of the framework—can indeed be attempted, and perhaps given, in psycho-physiological terms; but the very terms of the explanation belong to, or presuppose, that framework. As for the third variety I distinguished—the theory of logical construction, or the programme of definitional reduction—it would be hard now to find a single philosopher who retains any confidence in it. The difficulties of reduction came to seem insuperable—apart from the fact, already emphasized, that the concepts of material objects, obvious candidates for reduction, are themselves indispensable to a veridical description of the very sense experiences in terms of which they were to be defined.

So much, then, for that mentalistic, subjectivist tradition in philosophy which owes its origin, no doubt, to Descartes, but which, in a very different style, came to dominate the classical empiricism of Locke, Berkeley, Hume, and their successors. I have indicated the diverse ways in which philosophers of that tradition have tried to construct or justify or explain our general picture of the world on the too narrow basis of the succession of subjective mental states, including, above all, sense impressions; and have indicated the failure of these attempts. But there is another strand in philosophy which it is perhaps appropriate to mention now, since it incorporates almost an opposite—certainly a complementary error. If the first tradition might be called 'internalist', its opposite or complement might be called the thesis of externalism.[1] Internalism

---

[1] I am aware that the terms 'internalism' and 'externalism' have recently been appropriated in the service of discussion of a quite different issue. But I do not think that my usage of these terms here runs any risk of inducing confusion.

treats the inner subjective life of thoughts, sensations, and inner experience in general as a series of unproblematic private entities— and regards the physical world as problematic. Externalism treats the physical public world of bodies moving and interacting in space as unproblematic and the subjective and inner life as problematic. One form of internalism, as we saw, is reductionist or constructionist (it comes to the same thing): the problematic entities are to be reduced to, or constructed out of, the unproblematic entities. One extreme form of externalism has more or less the same programme— only the casting is turned upside down, the roles of problematic and unproblematic entities are reversed.

I shall not attempt a full diagnosis of the condition in which externalism is felt to be attractive. (It is perhaps felt to be the hard-headed or scientific approach.) Instead I shall content myself with two comments. One at least of the reasons for the attraction of externalism is certainly the thought that the characteristics, the relations, and the behaviour of bodies, including human bodies, in space are, or seem to be, satisfactorily definite and observable; whereas the mental or inner life seems to be characteristically elusive and indefinite, not available to public inspection or scientific verification. As we shall see shortly, when we seek a reply to the question, 'What is it to believe something?', we seem impelled to turn to the concept of *action*, hence movement in space, for a part of the answer. And similar perplexities beset us if we ask what it is to be struck by a thought or to experience a complex emotion. It is by no means an easy matter to keep our balance in these perplexities. But one thing that may help us not lose our balance in an externalist direction is to reflect on the very point I have just remarked on as one of the reasons for the attraction of externalism: the thought, namely, that the characteristics, the relations, and the behaviour of bodies, including human bodies, in space seem to be satisfactorily definite and *observable*.

Let us concentrate our attention on that last thought: *observability in perception*. Suppose we are surveying, observing some rich and complex physical scene; contemplating, perhaps, a stretch of the countryside. Then note that the perceptual experience of observing, of taking in, the scene is no less rich and complex than the physical scene itself *as we see it*. To try to effect an externalist reduction of the perceptual experience is not only intrinsically absurd; it is self-defeating; for it strikes at the very ground of the attraction of externalism itself: that is, the satisfactorily and definitely observable nature of the public, physical scene. So one useful corrective recipe for doubts about the inner is not to look within but to look without. The full and rich description of the physical world *as perceived* yields incidentally and at the same time a full and rich description of the subjective experience of the perceiver.

We can perhaps further heighten our sense of the absurdity of extreme forms of externalism about perception if we consider why people go to concerts or picture galleries. (One detects a shade of Philistinism in externalism.)

Now for my second comment. The impact of externalism is, of course, most immediately felt in the philosophy of mind and action. But it is not confined to the philosophy of mind—unless indeed we broaden our conception of the latter to include at least the philosophy of language, the theory of meaning, and the philosophy of logic. To take but one example of a ramifying effect. There is a distinction traditional in philosophy since at least the seventeenth century; Leibniz expressed it in speaking of the distinction between truths of reason and truths of fact. Other philosophers have spoken of logically or semantically necessary truths in contrast with contingent truths; or, perhaps more narrowly, of analytic and synthetic truths. When we assume, or strive to explain, these distinctions, we are apt to make a fairly free use of the notion of *meaning*, of the identity or inclusion or incompatibility of the *senses* of expressions, of the *propositions*, abstractly conceived, which sentences in use express, etc. Together with the notion of semantic necessity itself, these are all what Quine, for one, calls 'intensional notions' or 'intensions'. To the externalist-minded philosopher they are objects of suspicion; for they are, as Quine puts it, tainted with 'mentalism'. In contrast with them are what, from the externalist point of view, are respectable objects: outwardly observable events and objects, such as spoken or written tokens of sentences, and patterns of acceptance or rejection behaviour, in relation to combinations of linguistic expressions, on the part of speakers and hearers. It is unsurprising that we cannot, in these externalistically acceptable terms, plausibly reconstitute the distinction between the logically or semantically necessary and the logically or semantically contingent. But, for that very reason, we shall also recognize— unless we are under the spell of externalism—that these terms are inadequate to explain our own understanding of language. As language-users, we know what we mean by what we and others say well enough to recognize some inconsistencies and consequences, necessities and impossibilities, which are attributable solely to the meanings, the sense, of our words. And if these notions are indeed 'infected' with mentalism—and it is plausible to say they are—then a certain measure of mentalism is as inescapable in the theory of meaning as it is in the theory of perception.

Let that suffice on these two philosophical perversions: classical empiricism, or what might be called unbridled mentalism, on the one side and externalism, or what might be called unbridled physicalism, on the other. I return to the main project. Obviously there are general and fundamental traits of our system of ideas of which I have so far made no mention. I shall now briefly consider two of them. I shall not ask whether they are basic traits in the very strong sense of that expression—that is to say, whether they are absolutely indispensable to any coherent conception of experience. It is certain that they are basic or fundamental in the broader or more relaxed sense: that they are thoroughly pervasive of our thinking and intimately connected with other equally general notions already examined. Of the two features in question, the first is that we are agents, beings capable of action; the second is that we are social beings. The features are those of *agency* and *society*.

Let me recapitulate my sketch of our situation in the world as cognitive beings in order to bring it into relation with our situation in the world as active and social beings. I said: over time we build up a picture of the world in which we occupy at any moment a perceptual point of view; which extends in space beyond the range of that point of view; and in which we distinguish, under concepts of such things, space-occupying individual things which have, as we have, past histories and, perhaps, a future. What I want now to add is that this belief-picture of the world is not built up independently of our role as active beings.

Let us look first at the concept of action. Someone might ask: what makes the concept of action intelligible? And one might be inclined to answer: what makes the concept of action intelligible and brings our role as cognitive beings into relation with our role as agents is that we have attitudes of favour or disfavour towards states of affairs that we believe to obtain in the present or that we envisage as possible or likely in the future. Our beliefs matter to us, and that they should be true matters to us, largely because of these attitudes, because of what may broadly be called our desires and aversions. Our actions are based upon or issue from the combination of relevant belief and attitude; it is *as* issuing from such-and-such a combination of belief and attitude that an intentional action is the action it is. Our actions are directed towards the termination or avoidance of actual or possible future disfavoured states of affairs, and towards the perpetuation or bringing into being of actual or possible future favoured states of affairs; and they are thus directed in the light of our beliefs.

Let us call this the preliminary sketch of the position of the concept of action. It is all right as far as it goes. But it is inadequate in several respects. First, it does not sufficiently bring out the extent to which our concepts of space-occupying things in the world, and the very concept of our own perceptual position in relation to them, are permeated by the possibilities of action which they offer or inhibit. We do not, as it were, first learn what is in our world and how we are positioned in relation to what is in it and what changes or persistences are to be expected; and then, and independently, learn how we can modify things or our perceptual position in relation to them in ways which will conform as far as possible to our attitudes of favour and disfavour. The two kinds of learning are, rather, indivisible. In learning the nature of things, we learn the possibilities of action; in learning the possibilities of action, we learn the nature of things. Even the notion of our position and that of action are mutually dependent: what is *behind* me, for example, is essentially what I shall perceive, or bump into, if I *turn* or *move* in certain ways.

And there is no need to stress how much we learn of the world, at an early stage, by manipulation.

My concept of a door is a concept of that by the *action of opening* which I can pass into or out of a building or a room, and by the *action of closing* which I can exclude the sight or sound of what is on its further side.

We are aware of our situation in relation to things as bearing within it the germs of a future which is both limited and open. Our awareness of the situation as admitting certain possibilities of action is just the reverse side of our awareness of the limitation of those possibilities. Our concepts of things are concepts of things such that in relation to them we are in general neither omnipotent nor altogether helpless.

There is another respect in which the preliminary sketch of the concept of action is inadequate. It is not only the intimate connection between our concepts of objects and the concept of action that should be emphasized. There is an equally important link between the concept of belief and that of action. Action, as already remarked, flows from a combination of belief and desire; and can be, and has been, said to be caused by such combinations. But what we have here is not a simple causal relation beween things which are otherwise unrelated to each other. What is it, after all, to hold a belief? The question seems to have a particular force as regards our beliefs about what lies beyond our perceptual range at any moment. The reason for this I have already given in stressing the intimacy of the connection between perceptual experience and belief about the objective. Although, as I also mentioned, we may sometimes have special reasons for qualifying our judgement, there is in general a great deal of philosophical weight and value in the popular epigram: seeing *is* believing. And there is some philosophical value, too, in converting it to: *some* believing *is* seeing. That is to say, in the perceptual situation, the notion of believing seems to be flooded with content already, rich, as it were, with enjoyed experience. This cannot be the whole story even about such cases. But it cannot even be part of the story about those of our beliefs which relate to parts of the world which are not, so to speak, in view. So the question arises again: what is it to hold such a belief? Is it to entertain a thought or an image with a peculiar vividness, as Hume seems sometimes to suggest? Certainly not. One might thus conceive or imagine something which one strongly desired or greatly feared—without, however, believing in its reality. Or one might simply entertain oneself with vivid imaginings.

Neither will it do to say that we believe those propositions which we are prepared to affirm or assent to; for we must then add: provided that we speak in all sincerity, i.e. believing what we say. And this addition cancels the promised illumination. The circle, in this case, is much too narrow.

This is the point at which to recall the connection between our concepts of objects and our awareness of the possibilities of action which they offer. Given this connection, it follows that a belief about the world will often involve an awareness of possible ways of acting to avoid what one wishes to avoid and to achieve the ends one desires. So a first step towards the understanding of the concept of belief can be made by saying: to believe something, i.e. really to believe it, is, at least in part, to be prepared, if opportunity offers, to *act* in an appropriate way. This formulation is insufficiently exact. How to make the connection between *belief*, *desire*, and *action*, or preparedness to act, in exactly the right way is a problem which I commend, and leave, to you. But I can offer the following formulation which at least poses, or encapsulates, the problem in the right way: 'In men, or indeed in any rational being, the three elements of belief, valuation (or desire), and intentional action can be differentiated from each other; yet no one of these three elements can be properly understood, or even identified, except in relation to the others.'

From these sketchy remarks about the concept-user as agent I pass to some still sketchier remarks about the concept-user as social being. And I should like to call your attention to the extreme oddity of the procedure I have been following, in that I have so far made no mention of the fact that we are such beings. In a certain sense, indeed, it is not odd at all. That is, it has often been quite normal, quite conventional, in the philosophical tradition to work through epistemological and ontological questions in abstraction from the great fact of the concept-user's role as social being. All the same it is strange. For it is not as if each one of us builds up his cognitive picture of the world, acquires his concepts, develops his techniques and habits of action in isolation; and then, as it were, at a certain point, enters into relation with other human beings and confronts a new set of questions and problems. On the contrary. All this congnitive, conceptual, and behavioural development takes place in a social context; and, in particular, the acquisition of language, without which developed thinking is inconceivable, depends on interpersonal contact and communication. I have often used such expressions as '*our* conceptual system', 'the general structure of *our* thought', etc., in speaking of the basic or fundamental features of that system and that structure. One might well think it strange to use that human plural, 'our', without adding, and regarding as an equally basic feature of *our* scheme, that each must see himself in some social relation to others whose purposes interact with his. If our subject is man in his world, it seems necessary to admit that his world is essentially a social world.

Here we find ourselves at the threshold of philosophical questions in relation to which the concept of action and associated concepts have a quite particular poignancy: I mean questions of ethics and of political philosophy. But of these, with the exception of the question of free will and responsibility, I shall say nothing.

7

Truth and Knowledge

I TURN now to the notion of truth and its relations to the theory of knowledge and to the theory of linguistic meaning.

Historically, it is the first of these relations—the relation of the concept of truth to those of knowledge and belief—that has been the more prominent. It has sometimes seemed that what we were here presented with was essentially a field of debate between two conflicting theories of truth: the Correspondence Theory, according to which a belief is true if and only if it corresponds to a fact, an objectively existing state of affairs; and the Coherence Theory, according to which a belief is true if and only if it is a member of a coherent, consistent, and comprehensive system of held beliefs. The picture of an irreconcilable conflict between these views—of the concept of truth as offering a battlefield from which one theory must emerge as victorious with the other knocked out—may well strike us as implausible. We may be fairly confident that it is, rather, a matter of differently located emphasis—of emphasis on different parts or aspects of that system or interconnected ideas which constitute our conceptual system. What we need, then, is to assemble and relate some uncontroversial points; in Wittgenstein's words, to 'assemble reminders'. Here are some relevant platitudes.

1. The beliefs of each concept-user are partly based on *personal experience* of the reality his beliefs are about; perception and memory together contribute to building up his picture of the world. (Some beliefs are first-hand.)

2. A great part—indeed the more developed a concept-user's scheme of things, the greater that part—of a concept-user's beliefs

about objective reality are *not* based on personal experience of the objective reality the beliefs are about. Some of these not personally based beliefs come from the reports of others for whom they are personally based. A larger part, which come through all the media of instruction and communication, are not even, in this way, only second-hand. (Most beliefs are not first-hand.)

3. The concept-user's beliefs necessarily include general beliefs; for (*a*) concepts of objective things which preserve their identity through change, and which supply and fill the spatio-temporal framework of the objective world, are concepts of things which exhibit some regularity in their behaviour, and (*b*) the world could not be the theatre of goal-directed action without our having general beliefs which generate conditional expectations. (Some beliefs must be general beliefs.)

4. It must be possible for beliefs, or candidates for belief, to be in conflict with other beliefs. This is not simply because every proposition has a contradictory. More fundamentally, general concepts are essentially discriminatory. They usually come in ranges—e.g. the colour range, the temperature range, the animal species range—and thereby reflect the discriminations we make within the range, i.e. the application of one such concept in a given case is essentially incompatible with the application of some fellow-members of the same range. So particular beliefs, or candidates for belief, about the same thing may conflict with each other: such a belief, already formed, may conflict with a belief suggested by later experience or communication. Again, two particular beliefs which do not directly conflict with each other may generate conflict in the light of a certain general belief. Then, to restore consistency in the belief system we must give up either one of the particular beliefs or the general belief. (Beliefs may conflict.)

5. When candidates for inclusion in a concept-user's belief system are in conflict and he is aware of this, he may suspend belief on the question or resolve the conflict in favour of one of the conflicting candidates. The aim of consistency, or harmony, within one's system of beliefs is not simply an academic fad; for, as we have seen, one's beliefs about the world are inextricably bound up with one's practical involvement in it. So something at least approaching

consistency in one's system of beliefs is a necessary condition of the avoidance of intolerable stress and the achievement of effective action. (The need for consistency in beliefs.)

6. It is against the general background of a body of beliefs which as a whole is not in question at any given moment that the issue of whether or not to admit a new candidate, possibly at the cost of expelling an existing member, normally comes up.

All this seems uncontroversial. What is there to differ about? Yet, as remarked, the two 'Theories of Truth' I mentioned have seemed to be in conflict with each other. Perhaps we can see, instead, how each of the epitomizing slogans catches on to one aspect or another of the actual structure of our thought.

First, then, correspondence. This answers to a fundamental structural feature of our scheme, which I have been at pains to emphasize in the foregoing. That is, that reality indeed *contains* the enjoyment of experience and the forming and holding of beliefs; but that, in general, that in the world which an experience is an experience *of*, or a judgement or belief is formed *about*, is a reality independent in its existence of the occurrence of that experience of it or the formation of that judgement about it. This is reflected in the very concepts (of objects) which permeate experience and enter into judgement. So we generally conceive of the truth of a belief, whether it is experience-based or communicatively transmitted, as a matter of that independently existing reality to which the belief relates being *as* one who holds that belief thereby believes it to be. This is what is meant, and all that is (or should be) meant, by talking of the truth-relation of correspondence.

Second, coherence. Here the emphasis is largely, though not only, on the mutual dependence and logical interrelatedness of the beliefs which make up our systems of belief. The hostility is not really to the bare notion of correspondence as just described. The point is, rather, that to insist on this notion, on this platitude, by itself, can be misleading, in more than one way, if we want to get a realistic picture of our thinking, of our own picture of the world. First, it can be misleading if it encourages us to think of some beliefs as capable, as it were, of being separably, individually, and finally checked off, each against its own chunk of reality; and then, perhaps, to think of the whole structure as being merely compounded, with the help of the logical machinery of composition and generalization, out of, as it were, atoms of belief each of which by itself does have this simple checkable character.

More fundamentally still, the correspondence platitude may be misleading if it leads us to entertain a confused and ultimately self-contradictory picture of *concept-free* access to facts, to reality. Against such a picture, the Coherence Theory insists that you can have no cognitive contact with, hence no knowledge of, Reality which does not involve forming a belief, making a judgement, deploying concepts.

So we can see the Correspondence Theorist as insisting on a fundamental feature of any individual systems or structures of belief: viz. that they are systems or structures of belief *about* a reality conceived of as existing independently of those particular beliefs about it. And we can see the Coherence Theorist as insisting on the interdependence of the parts of the structure and on the point that you cannot correct one belief without forming another: insisting, in fact, that our structures of belief are *structures of belief*.

There is virtue in both insistences. More power to them both!

So much by way of a preliminary sketch of our topic. Now I want to approach the matter again, covering part of the same ground, but bringing out some refinements and qualifications ignored or glossed over in those preliminary remarks.

I take as my starting-point a truism about truth: more exactly, a certain simple schema or formula which everyone who discusses truth—whatever his theoretical position may be—is prepared to accept as valid or sound. If one chooses the letter 'p' to represent any position, the formula can be written thus:

> the statement/belief/conjecture (i.e. the proposition) that p is true if and only if p

or, more simply still,

> it is true that p if and only if p.

The formula seems to apply to all possible propositions, since any proposition is grammatically admissible in it. If someone *says* that John is bald, what he *says* is true if and only if John is bald. If someone *believes* that $7+5 = 12$, what he *believes* is true if and only if $7+5 = 12$.

Of course this schema or formula, though unassailable, is scarcely instructive. Its theoretical content is minimal. When philosophers raise questions about the nature of truth, they want something more substantial. Merely to write down the schema and add: 'All exemplifications of this scheme are valid'—that would scarcely count as a Theory of Truth. It is hardly surprising, then, that what philosophers offer us under the title 'Theory of Truth' often turns out to be either an investigation in the Theory of Knowledge or an essay in the Theory of Meaning—or even both at once.

I say this is unsurprising because clearly the notion of truth plays a central role in both these enquiries. On the one hand only what is *true* can be *known*; the conditions under which a belief can count as knowledge include, though they are not exhausted by, the condition that the belief is true. And, on the other hand, the notion of the condition under which a sentence expresses a truth (the notion of the truth conditions of a sentence) seems, on the face of it, central to the notion of the sentence's meaning. So the notion of truth serves as a link between the Theory of Knowledge and the Theory of Meaning. It is not the only link between them. The notion of *understanding* sentences provides another. It does so like this. A theory of meaning for a given language, if it is to have maximum interest and explanatory value, should not only show how the meanings of sentences are systematically determined by the meanings of their constituent elements and the ways in which they are combined (the constructions they exemplify). It should also give an account of how we understand meanings as so determined. A theory of meaning should be associated with or include a theory of understanding. But there would be something desperately wrong with claiming to understand sentences of a certain type while at the same time admitting that you had no idea at all what would justify you (or anyone else), in the case of any sentence of that type, in either asserting or denying such a sentence. But a general theory of the justifying conditions for affirming or denying propositions is just what has been traditionally understood as a theory of knowledge. So here is another link between the Theory of Meaning and the Theory of Knowledge. And if we think of understanding as grasp of truth conditions, we see that the two links are linked to each other.

There is nothing much to object to in these simple thoughts. And yet, in conjunction with our simple formula, they have the potentiality to mislead us in two quite different ways which I shall try to explain.

Let us consider again that simple-seeming schema or formula. It might appear to be not quite so empty as I suggested. Someone says, or believes, say, that John is bald. What he says or believes is true if and only if John is bald. Does not this formula at least make the point that, as J. L. Austin once expressed it, it takes two to make a truth? For the formula incorporates a twofold reference: a reference on the one hand to a believing or saying; a reference on the other hand to that in the world which the statement or belief is about. And it invites us to see the truth as consisting in a certain correspondence or fit between these two things. Moreover, in the case of a simple statement like 'John is bald', we can give a quite precise sense to this notion of correspondence or fit, as a relation between word and world. Such a statement fits the world—or its appropriate bit of the world—if the particular individual or item referred to by the subject term has the general characteristic assigned to it by the predicate term. Or, in other words: a statement which couples a particular name and a general predicate is true if and only if the named item satisfies the predicate. Of course not all statements are of this simple form. But any theory which sets out to show systematically how the truth conditions of sentences of more elaborate construction are determined by their constituent elements and their mode of combination must, it seems, be erected on the *basis* of just such simple forms as this. So it seems reasonable to believe that simple sentences of this type lie at the foundation of any semantic theory, i.e. any theory of meaning, for a given language.

And do they not also lie at the foundations of a theory of knowledge? The ability to recognize a particular individual, perceptually encountered, as possessing some general characteristic seems, on the face of it, fundamental not only to linguistic understanding, but also to knowledge in general. (I made this point long ago, in talking of the fundamental form of judgement.) And it is just the simple form of sentence we are considering which is best adapted to recording such recognitions (though, to be sure, that is not all that the simple form is fit for). It follows, perhaps, that we can represent the theory of knowledge and the theory of meaning as two aspects of a single theory, having a common base or point of departure, and yielding, between them, all that we can reasonably hope for by way of a substantial theory of truth.

Well, there is a bright and shining hope! But care is required. There is more than one way in which this bright prospect may lead us into error. One concerns the concept of truth itself. Another concerns that of knowledge. First, then, truth. With the aid of our simple example, I imagined someone finding it a merit of the simple scheme or formula we began with that it incorporated a twofold reference—to a saying or belief on the one hand, and to that in the world which the statement or belief was about on the other—and hence envisaging truth as a kind of word-to-world correspondence best understood in semantical terms. My first point is that an incautious commitment to this interpretation may involve the risk of either adopting too narrow a conception of truth on the one hand or of falling into what has often been plausibly represented as illusion or mythology on the other. We say, indeed, that John is bald; that $7+5 = 12$; that John ought to look after his sick brother; and so on. All these things we call true; and our thin formula, thinly understood, covers them all. But if we thicken our conception of truth to that of 'semantic correspondence between word and world', matters are not so straightforward. To be sure, we are in no difficulty with 'John is bald'. There is John, an object in the world, referred to by name, and visibly in a condition which satisfies or fails to satisfy the semantic condition for the truth of our statement. But what relations and dispositions of what things in the world make it true that $7+5 = 12$? Or, to take a truth of logic, the proposition that if John is bald, then John is bald, which is surely true whatever the condition of his head? Again, John and his sick brother are doubtless in the world: the former's activity of caring for the latter may or may not be so as well; but where in the world shall we find the relation signified by 'ought'?

There are at least two well-known responses to these difficulties, both of which show the power of the above-mentioned correspondence conception of truth. One is to declare that moral judgements, mathematical equations, and the tautologies of logic, since they do not appear to conform to the model, are not, strictly speaking, statements or propositions at all and hence are not, strictly speaking, true or false. They are to be assimilated, rather, to rules or imperatives. They relate to the ordinary natural world; but they relate to it, not as statements about it, but as instructions for action within it or for calculating or reasoning about it.

The other and opposite reaction is to embrace what is known as Platonism in mathematics and (perhaps) logic, and to accept the existence of 'non-natural' qualities or relations in the sphere of morals. The philosopher who follows this course does not, like his opponent, limit the concept of truth; instead he stretches or extends the concept of reality or the world. He imagines, or invents, or, as he would say himself, he recognizes, a realm of perfect, immutable mathematical objects of which the mathematician studies the nature and relations; or, as Moore did in the domain of morality, he imagines a layer of non-natural qualities or relations which supervene upon the qualities or relations to be found in nature, but require for their detection a special faculty of moral intuition.

Both reactions have been widely thought to be unsatisfactory. The first seems all too cavalierly to ignore or override the coverage of the concept of truth that we actually have. 'It is true that p if and only if p'—the unassailable formula that we began with—is no less hospitable to moral judgements and mathematical propositions than it is to records of common observation or history or propositions of natural science. At the very least this fact calls for explanation. The second reaction does indeed offer an explanation. But in the eyes of many this explanation has seemed spurious or hollow; and a spurious explanation is worse than none at all.

If both these reactions are unsatisfactory, and if they share a common presupposition it is that common presupposition which should be questioned. It is the simple model of word-to-world correspondence which encourages one party to confine the extension of the concept of truth within the limits of the natural world (as they conceive it) and encourages the other party to extend the concept of the world or reality to embrace all that is acknowledged as the truth. Of course I am not saying that we should give up altogether the simple model of word-to-world correspondence. On the contrary. I remarked long ago on the central role, in our system of ideas, of the distinction between our judgements on the one hand and, on the other, the objective reality which makes them true or false. So there are plenty of cases—perhaps the majority—to which the simple model applies in an unqualified way. Instead of abandoning the model, we should rather consider the kinds of case to which it applies without reserve as the primary or basic cases of truth; and then, taking this as a starting point, seek to explain how it is possible and legitimate to extend the notion of truth beyond these limits without feeding on myth or illusion. In this way one can succeed in understanding and accepting without difficulty the application of the notion of truth to propositions which are not simply records of natural fact, but play a different and perhaps more complicated role in our lives.

I spoke, however, of another way in which our earlier thoughts might mislead us. It is a question, this time, of the Theory of Knowledge. I spoke earlier of the capacity to recognize a particular situation or individual, encountered in perception, as being of a certain general kind or as possessing a certain general character; and I remarked that this capacity seemed fundamental both to linguistic understanding and to knowledge in general. Fundamental to linguistic understanding; for how else should the basic connections of meaning, the basic semantic links between word and world, be established? And fundamental to knowledge; for on what other basis could knowledge be developed, on what other foundation could the structure of beliefs which each of us counts as his knowledge of the world be erected?

Very good! It is well reasoned. And yet there is a danger, an insidious temptation, concealed in that metaphor of foundations: a temptation to which more than one philosopher has succumbed. Consider those propositions which, for any experiencing subject at any moment, are just the propositions which might serve as reports of the results of his exercise of this fundamental capacity of perceptual recognition; reports, that is to say, of current observation. Notice that I am not now speaking, in the classical empiricist style, of the subject's reports on his own subjective states, but of his observational reports on what currently lies before, or around, him in the world. It is these propositions which we are invited to consider as the foundations of knowledge.

But now we must ask what this means. We must ask what precisely is the doctrine which the metaphor of 'foundations' encourages us to accept. In the context of a particular argument or train of reasoning the metaphor of foundations has a clear sense. A man starts from certain explicit premisses and implicit assumptions and argues or reasons on this basis, to his conclusion. His argument really is a sort of structure which rests upon these premisses and assumptions. They are taken as accepted before the construction begins and they have to remain in place throughout the process. If one of them is knocked out, the structure is in danger of collapsing. In such a particular argument or chain of reasoning, then, there are indeed foundation propositions; propositions which serve as support for others and are not themselves at the moment regarded as in need of support.

However, it is clear that in such a context the foundation propositions are not just of one special kind; they may be of any kind. They may include general propositions; axioms of a theory; propositions about the remote past; truths learnt from other people or books; and so on. In this kind of context, propositions of current observation have no special privilege as foundation propositions.

Evidently, these points must be irrelevant to the doctrine we are to consider. It is not a doctrine about particular trains of reasoning. It is a doctrine about knowledge in general. It seems that it must be the doctrine that one special class of propositions, namely propositions of current observation, constitute the ultimate evidential support, the ultimate reasons (or grounds or justification) for our accepting as true everything else that we can properly, or correctly, be said to know.

But it is still not wholly clear what this means. One thing it might mean is the following: that when any person in fact *knows* some non-observation proposition to be true, then some observation proposition, or set of observation propositions, constitutes the reason, or the ultimate reason, which that person actually *has* for believing the non-observation proposition.

Unfortunately this is a quite preposterous thesis. It is only slightly less preposterous if one extends the class of observation propositions to include not only propositions stating what the individual currently observes, but also propositions stating what he can remember observing in the past. The thesis is preposterous in several ways. First, of all the things one knows, it is but an insignificant proportion of which one could truthfully say: my reason, or my basic reason, the reason I now actually have for believing this proposition, is such-and-such an observation or set of observations which I am either making now or can recall making in the past. Second, even when someone can cite an observation as his reason for believing some other proposition, it is normally a condition of its serving as a reason that the person in question should have other true beliefs which are not thus supported. (For example, my reason for believing at a certain moment that my petrol tank is empty, or nearly empty, may be my current observation that my petrol gauge reads zero. But my ability to make this observation, let alone appreciate its significance, depends on beliefs of mine for which current or remembered observation supplies no reason at all.) Finally, the thesis presupposes a picture of an individual's belief system which is itself a gross distortion of the facts of mental life.

That picture is one of a kind of hierarchical structure of beliefs, with higher members resting on lower members which are the individual's evidence for them or his reasons for believing them, and these lower members resting on still lower members until we come to the lowest level of all, the fundamental level. But it is quite false that an individual's belief system or set of beliefs is organized in any such way. This is not, of course, to say that the members of an individual's belief system lie entirely loose and separate in his mind, like items in a badly packed suit-case. On the contrary they are connected in numerous and complex ways. But they are not organized like an argument or an army of arguments. One could even say, of many propositions, that the more securely fixed they are in one's belief system, the less appropriate it is to ask what one's reasons are for believing them. What are my reasons now for thinking that my elder daughter's name is Julia, that the French for rabbit is 'lapin', or that Napoleon was defeated at Waterloo? Of course, I am not denying that I could produce or find reasons in support of these convictions if they were challenged. But it is not on the basis of such reasons that I now accept these propositions. I should like to say: there are things I know *too well* to have current reasons for believing them, too well to believe them *for reasons*.

As a picture of how an individual's belief system is organized in his mind, the thesis we are considering is, then, totally unrealistic.

Can we find for it any less unrealistic interpretation? It is often remarked that none of our beliefs about the world is in principle immune from doubt, from challenge or question; and when any one of our beliefs is seriously questioned, any rational procedure for settling the question will normally involve putting ourselves in a position to make some relevant observation. So observation propositions, it may be said, are at least the ultimate check-points of knowledge.

This is a more modest claim. Check-points are not foundations. Yet the impact of even this more modest claim is diminished once we realize that even the observational check-points cannot function as such without assistance of a quite different kind. Thus, first, as already indicated, many of the observations regarded as relevant to some disputed belief are observations that the observer could not even make, let alone appreciate the relevance of, were it not for the presence in his belief system of many other beliefs or assumptions which are not themselves in question at the moment of observation. Again, second, the function of relevant observation, in the case of disputed belief, is very often simply to give the observer access to the past or present *belief* of someone else regarded as authoritative on the matter in question. (You ask an authority or look up a text.) That the observation in such a case achieves the desired result is itself a belief involving a quite complicated set of further assumptions and beliefs. Finally, even granting that no proposition in our belief systems is in principle immune from doubt or question, yet we must note that any serious doubt or question, seriously raised in the spheres of history or natural science or practical affairs, presupposes an enormous framework or background of things taken to be known. In general, at any stage at which reasons are asked for, criticism is offered, conclusions are drawn, bodies of pre-existing knowledge or belief provide an indispensable background for these reflective operations; and it is only against such a background that observation propositions play their checking role.

Presumably we require of any theory of knowledge that it should give us a realistic picture of the general character of our knowledge structures and belief systems—including, or at least making room for, an account of how they develop and how they may rationally be modified. Such a picture must, of course, among other things, show how propositions of present and remembered observation *fit in* to the structure. So far the only truth about these propositions which we have been able to dig out from the ruins of the foundationalist metaphor is the rather specific platitude that when a seriously questioned belief is being checked, one has to make some observation, even if it is only a matter of looking at a text or listening to what someone says.

But there is one more general truth—I think a more poignant or interesting general truth—to be recovered from these ruins. Evidently the formation of the individual's corpus of belief—the formation of his world-picture—is the causal outcome of his exposure to, and interaction with, the world, including the instruction he receives from other members of his community; and evidently such exposure involves observation, seeing and hearing. At some point in this process there emerges the power of critical and self-conscious reflection. Perhaps we should not say that the individual has a body of beliefs before this power emerges. Certainly we should not say that this power emerges before he has a body of beliefs. Wittgenstein has well said: 'When we first begin to *believe* anything, what we believe is not a single proposition, it is a whole system of propositions. (Light dawns gradually over the whole.)'[1]

But the point to be stressed now is the ongoing and continuous character of the individual's exposure to the world. At any moment, we may say, our knowledge (or belief) system has to accommodate the beliefs which our current experience (our current observation) *forces on us* at that moment. This may, and generally will, involve no strain; and, as already implied, what our current experience does

---

[1] Wittgenstein, *On Certainty*.

force on us in the way of belief depends on the character of the pre-existent system. But the necessity of this kind of accommodation to current experience is a necessity which is always with us; and always was with us, from the time when we could first be credited with beliefs at all; so that, from that time onwards, all subsequent states of our belief system are the outcome of the ongoing process of accommodation to the unceasing pressures of experience.

These, then, are some modest elements of truth which we can and must retain from the ruins of the foundationalist thesis.

Let me be permitted to add that we can perhaps retain something else as well, something quite different: not a theoretical or philosophical insight; rather, a strictly practical precept: a caution against credulity; an encouragement to criticism; a reminder. Not every accepted belief or purported piece of information can be checked or tested against the evidence of our eyes and ears; but some can be and should be. A radical and all-pervasive (i.e. a philosophical) scepticism is at worst senseless, at best idle; but one of the things we learn from experience is that a practical and selective scepticism is wise, particularly when what is in question are the assertions of interested parties or of people with strong partisan or ideological views, however personally disinterested they may be.

✤ 8 ✤

Meaning and Understanding
Structural Semantics

M Y references to language and to the theory of meaning have so far been few and limited. I want now to discuss what has, of recent years, become a central issue in the philosophy of language.

Language, we say, serves for the expression of thought. More picturesquely, and more riskily, we may think of words and sentences as the clothing our thoughts put on when they make their appearance in public—or as the outward and visible (or audible) sign of the inward and spiritual thing. Pictures aside, it is surely right to say that, normally at any rate, speech and writing express thought; that sentences are significant only in so far as they have the power to do this. But if language in this way depends on thought, we must surely also feel the force of the idea that we do not have just a one-way dependence; that, at a level of any complexity, the availability in our language of a sentence for expressing a thought is, in general, a condition of the possibility of our thinking the thought. After a point—and with certain reservations about originality and the enrichment of language by the introduction of new concepts—after a point, and with these reservations, what we can't say we can't think. The thoughts must in general lie there, in potentiality, in the vocabulary and syntax of our language or languages. Yet, after that point, the thinking isn't just the speaking. We must *understand* our sentences. So here is one problem: the relation between thought and language. What does our understanding of our sentences consist in?

There is a particular part of this problem which has been very much to the fore in recent discussion. Consider again the idea of the thoughts lying there, in potentiality, in the language—in its vocabulary and syntax. Our language seems like a highly structured, autonomous realm of significance—yet a realm of which we are, in a sense, masters. It is *our* language. There are limitless sentences and combinations of sentences of which we know, in advance, the sense, the significance; though we shall only ever use, or hear, or read, a comparatively insignificant proportion of them. But even that insignificant proportion—which we do readily frame and utter, understanding what we say, or which we hear or read, understanding what we hear or read—even these are vastly numerous.

And so we ask: how is it that we have this vast and potentially limitless understanding? Clearly we do not learn the meaning of every new sentence independently. The whole point of the fact of the limitless potential is that we have no need to do this. So out of some limited means or material is generated this potentially limitless understanding.

Here we have a problem which has occupied many people working in the philosophy of language, and which is likely to continue to do so for some time to come. It seems at least plausible to hold that it must be solved by crediting us with (*a*) an implicit mastery (implicit in the sense of my original analogy with grammar) of a finite set of semantically significant constructions (general types of significant combination of linguistic elements) and (*b*) a grasp of a finite vocabulary of elements, which do have to be learned independently and individually; this mastery and this grasp being such that together they contain, and explain, the possibility of our limitless understanding. I said that this was a problem in the philosophy of language. And so it is. But surely, one may feel, it must, or might, be more. For if we could render explicit the structural principles which underlie our limitless linguistic understanding, would we not also be close to rendering explicit at least some of the general structural principles of all our thinking—given that interdependence of thought and language which I mentioned just now? So perhaps the analogy with grammar which I used originally has something in it which is more than just analogy.

But do not grammars vary enormously from one language to another? Certainly. So if our investigations are to have the universal significance we are being tempted to attach to them, we must see the variant grammars of particular languages as variant realizations of something more general—perhaps as variants on some abstract underlying structure expressing itself in different forms in different particular languages. Grammatical variation between languages is not, after all, an obstacle to their intertranslatability.

But where should we look for the general underlying structure? Remembering Quine's claims on behalf of canonical notation, we should not be surprised to observe that some philosophers at this point refer, or appeal, to formal logic. And, on a certain reasonable assumption, it is clear that logic does offer us at least a model of the sort of thing we are looking for. The assumption in question is the assumption that a central consideration in the understanding of sentences is a grasp of their truth conditions: to understand a sentence is to know what thought it expresses (or is capable, in given contextual circumstances, of expressing); and to know this is to know what we would be believing if we took that thought to be true. Now suppose we understand the notion of a true predication, of truly applying a concept in an individual case—a notion discussed earlier in these chapters. Then logic itself (or the semantics of logic, as displayed by Tarski) offers us a few simple recursive rules relating to quantification and sentence composition with the help of which we can generate an infinite number of sentences (or sentence forms) the truth conditions for which are shown to depend by these few simple rules on the truth conditions for the basic operation of predication. Of course, for this structure to have content, we must also learn the reference of individual names and the sense of individual predicates—the difference, for example, between the truth conditions for predicating 'blue' and those for predicating 'triangular'. But this will be so for any structural explanation. The point is that logic supplies an example of how grasp of a finite set of structural principles can yield grasp of a limitless set of structures.

And it may be thought (has been thought) to supply more; to

supply not merely a model of what we seek, but the necessary structural key to an adequate semantic theory for any natural language.

Now how could it do this? Well, suppose we could show that for all the semantically significant constructions in natural language we could find equivalent constructions which were already handled in standard logic. And suppose we could credit the user of natural language with an implicit grasp of these equivalences. Then it might be claimed that we have laid bare the structural principles our grasp of which explains our mastery of our natural languages—our understanding of a limitless range of sentences. So we have here a programme for reducing semantic structure in general to the structural forms so perspicuously displayed in standard logic; and this is sometimes thought of as revealing the true or deep logical forms of the natural language sentences—by a structural para-phrasing or recasting in the canonical forms.

It is worth remarking first that, as advocates of this programme would acknowledge, it is not free from internal problems and difficulties. Later, I shall suggest some more fundamental objections. But, for the moment, I shall content myself with a very simple example of an internal difficulty, i.e. of the sort of difficulty which confronts anyone who accepts the programme in principle.

Consider the two adjectives 'good' and 'bad' and an indefinite list of nouns such as 'footballer', 'lecturer', 'king', 'husband', 'designer', 'craftsman'. It seems clear that, in mastering the semantic force of the two adjectives, we have also mastered a very simple rule of combination and that, given that we know the meanings of the relevant nouns and have mastered the notions of predication and conjunction, we can put the right semantic interpretation on an indefinitely large class of sentences of which the following are instances:

(1) Charles I was a good husband and a bad king.
(2) John is a good designer and a bad craftsman.

But if we turn in a naïve spirit to formal logic to help us with the elucidation of the principles of our semantic understanding here, we are immediately in a dilemma. We cannot treat these sentences in the spirit in which we can treat many sentences which are superficially similar in form, such as:

(3) John is a 30-year-old footballer and a six-foot-tall lecturer.

This last we can treat as a conjunction of four simple predications, which could be redistributed in any order without affecting the truth value of what is said. To treat (1) and (2) in the same way would be semantically disastrous. It would lead for example to the result that (1) is equivalent, as regards truth conditions to:

(4) Charles I was a good king and a bad husband.

On the other hand, it would be equally unsatisfactory to say that in such phrases as 'good husband', 'good designer', etc. we have a set of predicates the meaning of each of which has to be learnt separately in each case, i.e. that there is no general rule which enables us to grasp the meaning of any such phrase given that we know the meaning of 'good' and of the relevant noun. Both these alternatives are quite unacceptable. And what is here shown about 'good' is true of an enormous range of other adjectives ('attributive adjectives', as they are called). Consider, for example, 'Jim is a slow thinker and a fast runner', 'Jumbo is a small elephant and a large pet', etc. So here we have one problem for the programme. And in general no simple manoeuvre stands the slightest chance of displaying as subject to the structural rules of logic all those structural features which are quite obviously at work in generating sentence meanings out of sentence elements. So the semantic theorist who is committed to this programme is bound to work hard at recasting whole classes of ordinary sentences in the attempt to reveal, or discover, what he will, if successful, regard as their true logical form.

These are internal difficulties. But even where they are, formally, overcome, there may remain objections of principle to the whole enterprise, objections which cannot be countered by any amount of ingenuity in paraphrase. I take another range of simple examples to illustrate the point. Consider the two sentences, 'John kissed Mary' and 'Tom died'. They appear to be, respectively, of the forms '$F(x, y)$' and '$F(x)$'; i.e. the first appears to consist of two singular terms and a two-place predicate, the second of one singular term and a one-place predicate. They are, evidently, typical of countless sentences used for reporting actions or events. Now consider the phrases 'in the garden' and 'at midnight'—typical adverbial phrases of time and place. Taking phrases and sentences together, we frame the slightly more complex sentences:

(1) John kissed Mary in the garden at midnight
(2) Tom died in the garden at midnight

which are themselves typical of countless sentences in which action or event reports are qualified by time- and place-adverbial phrases. They illustrate a type of construction which we understand very well and our understanding of which underlies our understanding of many such sentences. So long as we know the meaning or reference of the separate elements in the sentences, our understanding of the construction enables us to grasp the semantic force of the whole sentences; i.e. we do not have to learn, independently and separately, the meanings of the complex predicates, 'kissed . . . in the garden', 'died in the garden at midnight', etc.

Now part of our understanding of the construction consists in knowing that it follows from (1) that John kissed Mary at midnight and that John kissed Mary. Similarly for (2): it follows from (2) that Tom died. In general we know that we can validly infer the propositions obtained by dropping the time or place qualification or both from the affirmative propositions which contain them. The validity of these inferences cannot be represented in standard logic if we leave the sentences as they stand. Yet surely they are *structurally* valid. So the programme demands that they be recast; that semantically equivalent sentences be found which will display these inferences as validated by standard logic.

Professor Davidson has produced an ingenious solution to the technical problem presented by such sentences. The essential principle of the solution is to construe such sentences as referring to, by way of quantifying over, *events* and to construe the adverbial phrases as predicates of the events. This involves construing the main verbs of the original sentences as (or replacing them by) predicates which have one more place than they appear to have in their surface (or original) form, a place for events. Thus the apparent two-place predicate '. . . kissed . . .' appears as, or is replaced by, a three-place predicate, viz. '. . . was a kissing by . . . of . . .' and the apparent one-place predicate '. . . died' appears as, or is replaced by, a two-place predicate, viz. '. . . was a dying by . . .'. I will try to render the result in reasonably plausible English in each case. Thus for (1) we have:

(1') There was an event which was a kissing by John of Mary and which was in the garden and which was at midnight

and for (2) we have

(2') There was an event which was a dying by Tom and which was in the garden and which was at midnight.

These are respectively of the general forms '$(\exists x)$ $(F(x, a, b). G(x). H(x))$' and '$(\exists x)$ $(F(x, a). G(x). H(x))$' from which the inferences to '$(\exists x)$ $(F(x, a, b))$' and '$(\exists x)$ $(F(x, a))$' respectively are formally valid in the predicate calculus. So adverbial modification is reduced to predicate conjunction and the various inferences we know how to make are handled in standard formal logic.

One must admire the ingenuity of this proposal. On its own terms it is a success. But one may question the terms. I have already hinted at the existence of objections of principle, objections which the very ingenuity of such a proposal may serve only to underline.

The first objection to such a proposal is that it is unrealistic. It is unrealistic on the assumption that the point and interest of the exercise lie in its power to explain the language-speaker's capacity to understand a certain indefinitely large class of sentences. It seems indeed reasonable to credit the language-speaker with implicit mastery of principles of combination, of semantically significant constructions, in explaining his understanding of his sentences, even if he cannot readily articulate those principles. But it seems hardly realistic to credit him with implicit mastery both of the predicate calculus and of the transformation rules which license the paraphrase of the ordinary sentences into their Davidsonian replacements.

Not only does it seem unrealistic. It seems unnecessary. For, as I have emphasized earlier, it is a quite fundamental feature of our conceptual scheme that we conceive of the objective world as spatio-temporal and hence that we have the idea of places and times at which things happen or at which people act in various ways. We know that if Tom dies, he dies somewhere somewhen; we know that if John kisses Mary, they are somewhere when he kisses her and he kisses her at some time or other. What could be more simple and straightforward than the idea of a construction whereby we may tack on to the verbs of happening or action in such sentences a phrase which answers these when? and where? questions. The capacity to recognize such phrases *as having such a function* is all we need to be credited with by way of mastery of constructions and by way of explaining our grasp of the validity of the inferences in question. The thought that we need more, and in particular that we need a solution on the lines just considered, begins to look like a symptom of an unreasoned determination to force all (or as many as possible) of the structural semantic principles of combination which we understand into the framework of standard logic.

Earlier we noticed the need to invoke epistemological considerations as well as the fundamental logical duality (of individual and concept, reference and predication) in order to make progress in ontology or general metaphysics. Here we see the need to invoke general metaphysics in order to make progress in the philosophy of language. The mutual interdependence of what were cautiously distinguished as the three departments of ontology, epistemology, and logic (broadly conceived) is once more illustrated.

It might be said that the charge of lack of realism levelled against the particular proposal just considered is, at least, exaggerated. For, as my own rough paraphrases show, there can be framed, in more or less ordinary English, sentences which the ordinary language-speaker *will* understand as equivalent to the original sentences and which do approximate to the forms of standard logic required by Davidson's proposal. So where is the lack of realism in attributing to the ordinary language-speaker an implicit grasp of all this?

There is some force in this point. It takes some of the sting out of the charge that the explanation is unrealistic. But it leaves quite unaffected the charge that it is unnecessary. And it only takes some of the sting out of the first charge. Paraphrases on the models of (1') and (2') will typically introduce what the grammarians call nominal-izations—nouns or noun phrases formed from other parts of speech, in this case from verbs (e.g. the gerundial form 'a kissing' from the verb 'kiss'); i.e. generally, derivative or secondary forms. But it is taken to be part of the claim of the sort of theory we are examining that it *explains* our mastery of whole classes of ordinary sentences. And in the present case, if weight is really to be placed on the fact of the existence of reasonably intelligible sentences like (1') and (2'), this amounts to the claim that our ability to understand sentences like (1) and (2) *depends on* our ability to understand sentences like (1') and (2'). And this seems implausible in itself and the more so when the nominalized forms are derived from and secondary to the verb forms; i.e. when the latter come first in the order of understanding. I do not say the dependence claim is actually incompatible with this fact; for the claimed dependence might be understood as dependence not on actual, but on potential, understanding of the paraphrase forms. But in that case the claim of dependence has become so rarefied that its power to support the explanation claim is fatally attenuated—or so it seems to me.

A point of some interest, extraneous to the argument, but nevertheless worth mentioning, is this. Suppose one were ready to adopt Quine's criterion of ontological commitment, and his programme for determining what our ontological commitments really are: i.e. critical paraphrase into canonical notation, guided by the maxims of scientific acceptability and ontological economy (economy in respect of ranges of values of variables). And suppose further that one were also wholly convinced by the programme I have just been discussing, i.e. convinced that the revelation of the structural principles our mastery of which explained our mastery of our natural language was to be achieved only by the kind of paraphrase into the forms of standard logic which I have just illustrated—these paraphrases revealing the structure which we really at bottom understand our sentences as having. If you really held both these convictions, then the results of carrying out the programme would have for you a profound metaphysical or ontological significance. Thus acceptance of the Davidsonian analysis of action and event sentences would have a unique power to convince you that events and actions figured in our ontology; for they have to be reckoned among the values of our variables of quantification, they are quantified over, in the sentences which are held to reveal the underlying form of our ordinary sentences like 'Tom died' or 'John kissed Mary'. I draw your attention to this as an interesting—and, I am inclined to add, a slightly comic—curiosity; for surely we do not need any of these considerations and convictions to help persuade us that there are such things as events.

Finally, I must, in all fairness, say that some who view with sympathy the idea of the construction of a Theory of Meaning for a language on the lines I have been discussing (i.e. a theory for a natural language modelled on Tarski's Theory of Truth for a formalized language)—that some of these sympathizers do not claim for such a theory that it supplies, or, if completed, would supply, an explanation of our understanding of the constructions, hence of the limitless sentences, of our natural languages. They do not credit us with an implicit grasp of such a theory. Hence they do not think that to supply such a theory of meaning for a language would be to supply a theory of understanding. Hence the criticisms I have been making would not apply to them. But of course it must be added that the interest of the enterprise, as they conceive it, would be much reduced. For it would precisely not be a solution to, or even a contribution to solving, the problem we started out with—viz. how to explain our mastery of the limitless sentences of our language.

How, then, should we set about this problem? The question is a natural one, since the upshot, and indeed the purpose, of the remarks I have made so far have been largely negative. Well, I have already given a hint of an approach that would be at least partly in contrast with that which I have been describing and criticizing. Characteristic of the latter is its basis in purely formal and abstract notions of predication, truth-functional composition, and quantification—initially detached from the question of what types of concept and individual enter into our predications. The concern is with forms; and this reflects the characterization of logic as, in itself, indifferent to subject-matter. You are to think out, as you go along, how you have to fill the forms in order to meet the theoretical demands of the enterprise.

But suppose we began instead by concerning ourselves with the basic type of *matter* of our discourse and with the basic types of situation which we articulate in speech. Reflecting, as we have earlier been doing, on the basic features of man's situation in the world—which is, *au fond*, the same thing as reflecting on the basic features of his (our) conceptual scheme—reflecting that he is an acting, perceiving, corporeal being in a spatio-temporal world of other corporeal beings, including other men, all liable to change and mutual interactions, we may readily conceive that the basic categories in terms of which he thinks about his world will have a certain character; and that this will be reflected in the basic semantic types of element which will figure in his discourse and in the basic types of semantically significant combination of which they will be there susceptible. Nothing is said at this level about the actual linguistic forms, the grammatical structures, by means of which these combinations are represented, or in which they are, as we say, realized, in any actual natural language. But the hope will be that by identifying the forms in which the necessary combinations are in fact realized in a given language (or range of languages), we shall take at least the first steps towards the explanations which we are seeking; and we should not be surprised to find that the structures or forms we discover are more various than, though they include, simple predication, truth-functional composition, and the restricted styles of quantification recognized in standard logic.

Another result we might not unreasonably hope for is that of coming to appreciate how that part of the general grammatical structure which is abstracted in the logic of simple predication and quantification lends itself to application in more and more sophistic-ated types of discourse and of thought; so that we finally see logic itself, and the purely formal concepts of individual, property, relation, and identity as *emerging* in their unlimited generality as a result of progressive analogically extended application of certain features of the structure of basic utterances, i.e. of the sentences which relate to the basic types of subject-matter.

I have developed some of these thoughts a little way in a short book called *Subject and Predicate in Logic and Grammar*—particularly (as regards the first of the points just made) in what I there say about 'perspicuous grammars', as I call them; and (as regards the second) in what I there say about the generalization of the subject–predicate relation.

Along these lines we might make some progress towards the goal aimed at in the programme I have been criticizing. But I fear that this too is likely to remain more of a programme than a prospect; for its execution would call for an unexampled combination of linguistic knowledge, philosophical insight, logical expertise, industry, and perseverance.

✤ 9 ✤

Causation and Explanation

THIS chapter will be devoted to a somewhat more detailed examination of two related ideas which certainly figure among the key items of our conceptual equipment.

I

We sometimes presume, or are said to presume, that causality is a natural relation which holds in the natural world between particular events or circumstances, just as the relation of temporal succession does or that of spatial proximity. We also, and rightly, associate causality with explanation. But if causality is a relation which holds in the natural world, explanation is a different matter. People explain things to themselves or others and their doing so is something that happens in nature. But we also speak of one thing explaining, or being the explanation of, another thing, as if explaining was a relation between the things. And so it is. But it is not a natural relation in the sense in which we perhaps think of causality as a natural relation. It is an intellectual or rational or intensional relation. It does not hold between things in the natural world, things to which we can assign places and times in nature. It holds between facts or truths.

The two levels of relationship are often and easily confused or conflated in philosophical thought. They are confused in philosophical thought partly because they are not clearly distinguished in ordinary or non-philosophical thought. And they are not clearly distinguished in ordinary thought because making the distinction would often serve no practical purpose. Nevertheless, in so far as our philosophical purpose is to understand our non-philosophical thought, it is well that *we* should be aware of the distinction.

It is easy to point to evidence that the distinction is not clearly marked in ordinary speech. We use nominal constructions of the same general kinds—nouns derived from other parts of speech, noun clauses, gerundial constructions—to refer both to terms of the natural and to terms of the non-natural relation. We use the same range of expressions (for example, 'cause' itself, 'due to', 'responsible for', 'owed to') to signify both the natural and the non-natural relation; or use these expressions in such a way that we may be hard put to it to say which relation is specified and thus perhaps be led to doubt whether any such distinction exists to be drawn. This is not to say that we are always at a loss as to which relation is being specified. Faced with a remark of the form 'The reason why *q* was that *p*' (for example, 'The reason why the building collapsed was that it was constructed of inferior materials') or of the form 'The fact that *q* is accounted for by the fact that *p*' ('The fact that the building collapsed is accounted for by the fact that it was constructed of inferior materials'), we need be in no doubt that it is the non-natural relation that is in question; whereas we are left in doubt by 'The collapse of the building was due to/caused by the use of inferior materials in its construction' or by 'The use of inferior materials in the construction of the building was responsible for its collapse'.

There are sometimes relatively subtle indications of difference. Thus we might compare 'His death, coming when it did, was responsible for the breakdown of the negotiations' with 'His death's coming when it did was responsible for the breakdown of the negotiations'. His death, as referred to in the first of these sentences, is certainly an event in nature. It came when it did. But his death's coming when it did did not come at any time. It is not an event in nature. It is *the fact* that a certain event occurred in nature at a certain time. Are we then entitled to conclude that the phrase 'the breakdown of the negotiations' refers, in the first sentence, to an event in nature and, in the second, to the fact that that event occurred at a certain time, and that the phrase 'responsible for' signifies, in the first sentence, the natural and, in the second sentence, the non-natural relation? We are not entitled to draw any such conclusion. For it simply need not be true of the ordinary language-speaker either that he means to speak consistently at one level or the other or that he mixes levels. It is often simply that he does not distinguish levels, because he has no need to.

An exhaustive examination of ordinary usage on this point would be a possible exercise and one neither uninteresting nor unprofitable. But it is not, I think, indispensable. So I shall forgo it.

A little more must be said, however, of a preliminary kind, about the distinction I have drawn, or suggested, between the putatively natural relation of causality, said to hold between things in nature, and the non-natural explaining relation, said to hold between facts or truths. The latter description may seem obscurantist or at least provocative. I do not mean, in adopting it, to deny any connection between this relation and natural facts. On the contrary, my aim is to emphasize a certain connection with certain natural facts, namely, natural facts about our human selves. As a first approximation, one could say that the non-natural fact that the explaining relation holds between the fact that p and the fact that q expands into the natural fact that coming to know that p will tend, in the light of other knowledge (or of theory) to induce a state which we call 'understanding why q'. The non-natural relation between the truths is mediated by the connection which, as a matter of natural fact, we give them (or they have) in our minds. This is why, as a variant on calling the relation non-natural, I called it rational. But the objects so related are obstinately intensional objects, not assignable to a place or time in nature, though of course the thinking of them, the reporting of them, and the objects they are about may all be so assigned. (Since the objects related by the explaining relation are not found in nature, the relation between them is not found in nature either: the relevant natural relation is between events in our minds. But we cannot report *these* naturally related events without reference to the non-naturally related objects.)

Against this it has of course been said that facts are part of the natural world, forming a rather comprehensive category which includes events, conditions, and the like. Linguistic evidence can be called on both sides of this debate. But it is not a very profitable debate except in so far as it makes us aware, once more, of the absence of practical need to mark clearly and consistently a distinction which it nevertheless behoves *us* to draw. Once this is recognized, the debate itself can be amicably and trivially terminated by each side allowing the other some rights in the word.

Once we are clear about the distinction I am drawing, we can avoid certain tangled ways of speaking which seem to have gained currency in recent philosophical writing. Thus we sometimes read of an event 'under such-and-such a description' being the cause—or being the explanation—of some other event or state-of-affairs. But both these ways of talking, whether of cause or explanation, must be quite confused if there is in truth such a distinction as I have drawn. Suppose a particular happening or a particular condition of things, *A*, is the cause or part-cause of another particular happening of things, *B*. Then if causality is a natural relation, a relation which holds in nature between *A* and *B*, that relation holds however *A* and *B* may be described. Of course it is not true that we can choose any uniquely applicable descriptions of *A* and *B* that take our fancy and still be confident that the fact that there occurred or existed an event or condition answering to our chosen *A*-description will explain the fact that there occurred or existed an event or condition answering to our chosen *B*-description. If what we are after is an explanation, we must select appropriate facts about *A* and *B*. Selecting an appropriate fact about an event or condition may involve choosing among different possible descriptions of the same event or condition. It does not involve choosing among different descriptions of the same fact. The fact is, in this connection, something to be stated, not described.[1] So whether what is at issue is the reporting of a causal relation or of an explaining relation, it is misleading, and a mark of confusion, to say that one thing, under such-and-such a description, either causes or explains another. If the distinction I have drawn is sound, the situation is, rather, first, that *A* causes *B* *simpliciter*; and, second, that the truth of some statement including some description

---

[1] Though it is, of course, possible to describe facts; as when we say of some fact that it is widely known or insufficiently appreciated.

of *A* explains the truth of some statement including some description of *B* (or, in other words, that some *A*-involving fact explains some *B*-involving fact).

But then what makes descriptions suitable to figure in such statements? Or, in other words, what makes the selected facts the right facts to stand in the explaining relation? And what is the connection between the suitability of the descriptions, the rightness of the facts, and the causal relation itself, the relation which, we presume, holds in the natural world, when it does hold, between particular events and conditions, however described? Surely there must be such a connection. Surely the power of one fact to explain another must have some basis in the natural world where the events occur and the conditions obtain and the causal relations hold. We must think this on pain of holding, if we do not, that the causal relation itself has no natural existence or none outside our minds; that the belief in such a relation is simply the projection upon the world of some subjective description of ours, the disposition, perhaps, to take some facts as explaining others.

Now this is, in part, the doctrine that Hume is generally thought to have held, though the subjective disposition he saw as thus projected was different from that just mentioned. But of course this was, at most, only a part of his doctrine. For he also held that there was indeed a natural basis which existed independently of the disposition in question, a basis for that disposition to operate on. Only this basis was not something that was intrinsically capable of being detected or observed or established *in any particular case*. It was only the observation of the repeated holding, in like particular cases, of certain other relations which *were* intrinsically capable of being detected in the particular case, that could ground the attribution of the causal relation, in any one individual case, as something holding irrespective of any subjective disposition of ours. So the causal relation regarded as holding between particular 'objects' (as Hume would call them) has, on this view, a quite unique character; it is a dependant of generality; it is not, one is tempted to say, something actually present in the particular situation involving the particular objects at all. Or, to put the point in another way, causal generalizations are not generalizations of particular instances of causality; rather, particular instances of causality are established as such only by the particularizing of causal generalizations.

This famous and ingenious solution has become and, in spite of later sophistications, has in essentials remained what the greatest of Hume's critics called 'the accepted view'. It may be worth repeating that critic's summary of the accepted view. It is, he says, the view 'that only through the perception and comparison of events repeatedly following in a uniform manner upon preceding appearances . . . are we first led to construct for ourselves the concept of cause'.[2] Never mind that this summary omits the boldest elements in Hume's doctrine, namely his diagnosis of the source of the belief in necessary connection in nature; for that diagnosis has not generally found favour and forms no part of the view as generally accepted.

The received view has not been universally received. It has been attacked from different angles. Kant's own counter-argument, where clear, is clearly unsuccessful; and indeed it seems to me that no direct attack, no attack which concentrates on the highly general notion of cause, or on that of necessity, is likely to be successful. Nevertheless there is a family of points, none of them novel, which, rightly organized, may radically change the face of the received view, and put it, as it were, in its place. I am fairly sure that I have not succeeded, in what follows, in finding the right organization of these points. Nevertheless I shall assemble them; or some of them.

II

Before I begin to assemble these points, it will be well to indicate the general line I propose to follow. The received view, I shall maintain, is partly right and partly wrong. It is true that there is no single natural relation which is detectable as such in the particular case, which holds between distinct events or conditions and which is identifiable as the causal relation. Neither is there a plurality of relations observable in particular cases, holding between distinct events or conditions and identifiable as specific varieties of a general

---

[2] Kant, *The Critique of Pure Reason*, B 240-1.

type of relation, namely the causal. In this respect, the notion of causality differs from another categorial notion, that of an individual substance, with which it is traditionally, and rightly, associated. Both notions are highly abstract. Neither belongs to the vocabulary of particular observation. But whereas there is a host of expressions for specific kinds or varieties of individual substance which do belong to the vocabulary of particular observation—so that of particular dogs and tables, men and mountains, one can say that each is an observable instance of such a kind—there is no evident parallel for this in the case of causality, *thought of as relating distinct particular events or circumstances.*

On this negative point, then, the traditional view is justified. But it is a grave error to attach to this negative point the importance that traditionally attached to it. It is a grave error to take this negative point as a starting point in the elucidation of the concept of cause. It is the error of premature generality. Though the notion of cause, *understood as a relation between distinct particular events or circumstances,* finds, in the observation vocabulary, no footing which exactly parallels that which I have just illustrated in the case of the notion of substance, yet the notion of causation in general does find a footing or, rather, a foundation, and a secure foundation, in the observation vocabulary. There is an enormous variety, a great multiplicity, of kinds of *action* and *transaction* which are directly observable in the particular case and which are properly to be described as causal in so far as they are varieties of *bringing something about,* of producing some effect or some new state of affairs. The absence of parallel, previously remarked on, with the case of substances is easily explained; for when, as often, in reporting such observable actions or transactions, we employ a two-place predicate, a transitive verb appropriate to the type of transaction in question, the two places are not filled by the designations of distinct particular events or circumstances. At least one of them is filled, and often both are filled, by the designations of particular substances. Typically, though not exclusively, such a predicate signifies some specific exercise of causal power by an agent, animate or inanimate; and often, though not always, an exercise of such a power *on* a patient.

Nothing, then, could be more commonplace than the observation, in particular cases, of specific varieties of the bringing about of effects by things. The observation vocabulary is as rich in names for types of effect-producing *action* as it is in names for types of substances. Indeed the two kinds of name—for types of substance and types of action—are indissolubly linked with each other. Thus one thing, say, acts to bring about an effect, a new state of affairs— perhaps in another thing—by a characteristic exercise of causal power; and in observing such a transaction one already possesses the explanation (or at least the immediate explanation) of the new state of affairs. There is no question of dissolving the transaction into a sequence of states of affairs—a sequence of 'distinct existences'— and wondering whether, or in virtue of what, the sequence constitutes a causal sequence. One has *observed* the change being *brought about* in some characteristic mode. Someone who observes the outcome, but not its bringing about, may seek an explanation of the outcome; and to him the outcome can be explained by mentioning the observable, but by him unobserved, action of bringing about the outcome. In these cases, then, the explanation rests directly on observable relations in nature.

But, of course, explanation is not always so easily had. And when it is not, there begins, or may begin, the search for causes; guided partly by those models of bringing about, of the exercise of causal power, which nature presents to gross observation, and partly by that observation of regularities of association of distinct existences which is dear to the holder of the received view. If, by theoretical construction or minuter observation we can discover or postulate copies or images or analogies of our grosser models to link the mere regularities of conjunction, then we are satisfied, or provisionally satisfied, that we have reached the level of explanation; that we have found the cause. Even in those cases where the observation vocabulary supplies us with verbs of action or undergoing, so that in a sense we already understand effects by observation of their grosser modes of production, we may have motives for seeking a deeper, or more general, understanding and hence for investigating the micro-mechanisms of production, the minuter processes which underlie the grosser. It is true, no doubt, that in the evolution of sophisticated physical theory, the use, and the utility, of our grosser models diminishes and finally, perhaps, wears out altogether. At this point also the notion of cause loses its role in theory; as Russell said that it would and should. But that is a point which none of us occupies for much of the time and few of us occupy at all.

III

Now to start to fill in this outline. Hume tracked down to a subjective source what he took to be the distinctive feature of our conception of causality as a natural relation. That distinctive feature he usually referred to as the idea of necessary connection. But he allowed that it bore other names of which he said that they were virtually or, as he put it, 'nearly' synonymous. His list of nearly synonymous terms includes 'efficacy', 'agency', 'power', 'force', 'energy', 'necessity', 'connexion', and 'productive quality',[3] to which he might have added 'compulsion' without straying far outside the bounds of his notion of near-synonymity. In tracking the idea down to its subjective source he of course followed, or claimed to follow, his leading principle: seek the impression from which the idea is derived. But, curiously enough, in the *Treatise* Hume ignored the most obvious direction in which that principle might have led him. If we concentrate on the trio 'power', 'force', and 'compulsion', and ask from what impression the idea discernible in them all is derived, the most obvious answer relates to the experience we have of exerting force on physical things or of having force exerted on us by physical things—including here the bodies of other people as physical things.[4] We push or pull, or are pushed or pulled, and *feel* the pressures or the tugs, the force, compulsion, or power that we exert or have exerted upon us. Here is as immediate an experience as could be desired: an impression of force exerted or suffered. (The very word 'impression' has here its own ironical resonance.) In a dismissive footnote in the *Enquiry*[5] Hume appears to respond to the

---

[3] Hume, *A Treatise of Human Nature*, I. iii. 14.
[4] The point is elegantly made by Austin Farrer. See *The Freedom of the Will* (London, 1960), 184.
[5] *An Enquiry concerning Human Understanding*, VII. ii, final footnote.

point by seeking to atomize the total experience: isolating a pure bodily sensation as a single element merely accompanying, succeeding, or preceding other simple impressions of sense. But so to atomize is to falsify; as Hume systematically falsifies the phenomenology of perception in general.

Here then is a source of one of the ideas which Hume scornfully links together as 'nearly synonymous'. Of course, however, we do not limit the application of the idea of force to those mechanical transactions, those pushings or pullings, in which we ourselves, or our fellows, are engaged as agents or patients. We extend the idea to all such transactions. Is there, as Hume suggests in the footnote referred to, an element of anthropomorphic projection in this extension? Perhaps so. In a great boulder rolling down the mountainside and flattening the wooden hut in its path we see an exemplary instance of force; and perhaps, in so seeing it, we were, in some barely coherent way, identifying with the hut (if we are one kind of person) or with the boulder (if we are another): putting ourselves imaginatively in the place of one or the other. But whether or not such an element of projection underlies, or lingers on in, the extended application of the notion is a matter of no consequence. For the point is that in these mechanical transactions, these pushings and pullings or knockings down or over, these manifestations of force, we have examples of actions, of natural relations, which, whether entered into by animate or inanimate beings, are directly observable (or experienceable) and which, being observed (or experienced) or appropriately reported, supply wholly satisfactory explanations of their outcomes, of the states of affairs in which they terminate. We see the boulder *flatten* the hut. The outcome is the state of the hut, the state of being flattened. We see the man *pick up* the suitcase and *lift* it on to the rack. That is the explanation of the suitcase's being on the rack; that is how it got there.

I am suggesting, then, that we should regard mechanical transactions as fundamental in our examination of the notion of causality in general. They are fundamental to our own interventions in the world, to our bringing about purposed changes: we put our shoulders to the wheel, our hands to the plough, push a pen or a button, pull a lever or a trigger. Entering into them ourselves, we find in them a source of the ideas of power and force, compulsion and constraint. Ourselves apart, they include observable natural phenomena, actions or relations directly detectable in the particular case, the observation of which supplies explanations of the states they end in. Finally, much of the polymorphous language of gross causal action and relation falls into this category: as 'push', 'pull', 'lift', 'put', 'remove', 'open', 'close', 'bend', 'stretch', 'dent', 'compress', and so on.[6] It is not then to be wondered at that such transactions supply a basic model when the theoretical search for causes is on; that we look for causal 'mechanisms'; that, even when it is most clearly metaphorical, the language of mechanism pervades the language of cause in general, as in the phrases 'causal connection', 'causal links', and 'causal chain'.

Consideration of the notions of attraction and repulsion, fundamental in physical theory, confirm this claim. In the first place, the sense of mechanical interaction as being paradigmatically explanatory goes a long way to accounting for an initial reluctance to accept the idea of action at a distance, and the associated inclination to posit some medium through which impulses are transmitted. Second, even when the reluctance is overcome, it is still the model of pushing and pulling which is indirectly at work. There is indeed a double indirectness here. For though the presence of the push-pull notions is etymologically obvious in the words 'attraction' and 'repulsion', the application of these words in the case of physical action at a distance is surely mediated by their already analogical application in the case of beings capable of desire and aversion who are said to be 'drawn to' or 'repelled by' the objects of these emotions. The French word for magnet, after all, is *aimant*.

Closely connected with the model provided by the mechanical interaction of solid bodies is that supplied by the behaviour of fluids. This again pervades the figurative language of cause in general, as when we speak of the *sources* from which consequences *flow*. More specifically, it provides a preliminary model in the theory of *current* electricity: current *flows* under *pressure*, encounters *resistance*, and so on.

[6] Cf. G. E. M. Anscombe, 'Causality and Determination', reprinted in Ernest Sosa (ed.), *Causation and Conditionals* (Oxford, 1975), 63–81.

In general, then, the search for causal theories is a search for modes of action and reaction which are not observable at the ordinary level (or not observable at all, but postulated or hypothesized) and which we find intelligible because we model them on, or think of them on analogy with, those various modes of action and reaction which experience presents to gross observation or which we are conscious of engaging in, or suffering ourselves. Such a statement calls for qualification. I do not wish to draw too sharp a line between observation and theory. Refined observation will notice powers and propensities which grosser observation passes over. Refined observation shades into theory. Again, one theory may itself provide the basis of analogy for another; as the gravitational theory applied to the solar system supplied the model for a theory of subatomic structure. And finally, as already suggested, in the most sophisticated reaches of physical theory the models seem to wear out altogether. Equations replace pictures. Causation is swallowed up in mathematics.

IV

In making, as I have done, so direct a transition from the topic of observable production of particular effects to the topic of the search for general causal theories, it may seem, and with reason, that I have passed too quickly over too much. For, it may be said, it is vital to distinguish between the theoretical enquiry into the causes of some general phenomenon and the demand for explanation of the occurrence of some particular incident or the obtaining of some particular state of affairs; and the mere reference to the observable production of effects constitutes no adequate treatment of the latter topic even in those cases where such observation of causal action is available.

There is point in this. For though some observable production of an effect, by some particular manifestation of causal power or liability, may yield an immediate explanation of the effect, there is often still room for the question why that particular manifestation occurred, why the type of which it was an instance was then and there realized. To meet the point, it is necessary and sufficient to return to the topic of concepts of types of substance and their link with concepts of types of action and reaction (or of obstruction or resistance to action). The existence of the link—the thoroughgoing dispositionality of our substance concepts—is a philosophical commonplace. Yet such is the persisting power and influence of the Humean theory of causation that the importance of this common-place in its bearing on that topic is regularly missed or underrated.

Our concepts of types of individual thing or substance, then, are concepts of things with characteristic dispositions to act or react in certain ways *in certain ranges of circumstances*. Emphasizing that last phrase, we might say, with pardonable exaggeration, that all action is reaction. But of course we may observe or learn of some action or reaction of a thing without knowing which of a characteristic range of action- or reaction-triggering circumstance operated in a particular case; or without knowing the details of those circumstances; or without knowing enough of the surrounding circumstances even to be able to choose a satisfactory classification of the observed behaviour from among those types of behaviour to which substances of the kind in question are prone. In all these cases a demand for explanation is in order. This is a demand for the filling-in of gaps in our knowledge. But the gaps, one is tempted to say, are like blanks in an already prepared proforma. We know in advance the range of possible fillings; for we know what type of thing we have to deal with. It is not that we first acquire the concepts of types of thing and only then, and only by repeated observations of similar conjunctions of events or circumstances, come to form beliefs about what kinds of reaction may be expected of such things in what ranges of antecedent conditions. Rather, such beliefs are inseparable from our concepts of the things.

It will not do to exaggerate the scope of the point; nor have I exaggerated it—or at least not greatly—in the formulation just given. It would be absurd to deny, and I have not denied, that we learn by experience, as we say, about the propensities of things of different types and, indeed, about the propensities of individual specimens of those types; most notably the latter when the type is the type of fellow human beings. But the learning takes place in a pre-existing, in an already prepared, framework of conditional expectation. There is no point, in our self-conscious existence as beings aware of a world of objects and events, at which we are equally prepared, or unprepared, for anything to come of anything; and hence no process, whereby we emerge from this condition, such as that described by Hume: observation of constant conjunctions generating mental compulsions which we then project upon objects in the form of the delusive notions of efficacy, agency, power, force, necessary connection, and the like.

But surely, it might be said, it is at least true that it is the observation of regularities which suggests or confirms that enriched conception of the powers or propensities of things which we owe to experience? No doubt there is truth in this. But it goes no way to show that the notion of causal action or reaction, as embodied in the myriad specific forms which it takes in our common and theoretical vocabularies, is derived from experience of bare regularities of succession or that it is, as far as all objective content is concerned, reducible to such regularities—the idea which Hume first sketched and which Mill and subsequent writers have refined. To think that such a derivation is necessary or possible is to get things the wrong way round. And to see this it is sufficient to bear in mind two points already suggested or explicitly made.

The first is, once more, the thoroughgoing dispositionality of our ordinary pre-theoretical concepts of things and their qualities. With this dispositionality, the *generality*, which is the core of the reductive conception, is already given. It is not given in a form which supplies any comfort to the reductionist. This it could do only if the relevant concepts of thing and quality dissolved into, or were constructed out of, a complex of wholly non-dispositional concepts (of sense-quality) plus generalizations relating them. But the relevant concepts of thing and quality do not so dissolve and are not so constructed. They are basic conceptual stock; and to think otherwise is to misrepresent us as theorists before we have the means of theorizing. It is internal, then, to the relevant concepts of thing and quality, the concepts which belong to our basic, pre-theoretical stock, that those things, or the bearers of those qualities, regularly act and react in such-and-such ways. *This* is the conceptual setting in which dispositionality carries generality within it. It is on this basis that observation of regularities can help us to enrich our primitive conceptions of the powers and propensities of things—those primitive conceptions without which we would have no conception of the things themselves. And this is why the received or traditional account of causal action and reaction can, with unusual aptness, be said to put the cart before the horse.

Or, rather, that is one reason. The other, also previously suggested, is that mere regularities of succession do not of themselves satisfy us that we have found causes. The symptoms displayed at successive stages of a disease may exhibit as high a degree of regularity as could be desired. The birds flying inland portend the coming storm. Many other phenomena are quite reliable indications of yet other phenomena to come. But it is only if we can more or less dimly conceive of the antecedent and the subsequent phenomenon as being connected in some way more or less remotely assimilable to, or analogous to, the models of causal action and reaction which we already possess, that we are disposed to regard the former as the cause of the latter. To those of a more curiously enquiring turn of mind—to the *natural* natural scientist—such a dim and vague conception of a causal link will not be satisfactory. He wants to know the detail of the link, the inner mechanism of the connection. He wants to know *how* it works. Only then is he satisfied that he possesses a full understanding of the matter. Not, of course, that the interest in such understanding is purely theoretical. For it is by means of these enquiries that we extend our own control over nature, our own power to bring about or avert effects that we desire or fear.

The general point I have been urging in the immediately preceding paragraphs is that, though we do indeed learn much about the operation of causality in the world through the observation of regularities of succession, we do so only because the general notion of causal efficacy and causal response, of effects being brought about in a variety of specific ways, is already lodged with us, is already implicit in a wide range of concepts of thing, quality, action, and reaction which belong to our basic stock of concepts of the observable. This is why Kant is fundamentally right against Hume; although, partly because he also shared the almost universal fault of treating the topic at an excessively high level of generality, his particular arguments are defective. Nevertheless, he had a secure grasp of the central point, which it would perhaps not be unacceptable to express in more or less his own words by saying that the concept of causal efficacy is not derived from experience of a world of objects, but is a presupposition of it; or, perhaps better, is already with us when anything which could be called 'experience' begins.

V

I remarked earlier that the notion of mechanical action, directly experienced or observed, and the more general and indirectly derived notion of physical force (attraction and repulsion) play a fundamental part in the elaboration of causal theories. They provide models of the explanatory. But at an early stage of human theorizing we find another model at work. (The supplementary model is itself connected with the mode of derivation which I suggested for the generalized notions of physical attraction and repulsion.) I refer to the model of human action and motivation. It is not by reliance on an observed constant conjunction between motive and movement that we know why we arc acting as we do act. Any such idea is quite absurd. We have, in general, immediate knowledge of what we are up to, of what we are doing or trying to do. Such knowledge is a species of immediate causal knowledge: knowledge of our desires and aims as moving us to try to fulfil or achieve them. In so far as we can assign any effect in the world to the act of an agent, himself (or herself) actuated by such motives as we know in ourselves, we feel that we can to that extent understand it. In so far as we can conceive certain effects, desired or feared by us, to be within the power of certain agents, we also conceive it to be within *our* power to influence the production or avoidance of those effects to just the extent to which we can supply those agents with appropriate motivation. Our primitive, and not so primitive, theorists, aware of their own powers of agency and of the motives behind their exercise, aware, also, of vast effects in nature, dreaded or hoped for, but quite beyond their own powers directly to avert or produce, seem to have found it utterly easy and natural to attribute these effects to the exercise of powers by superhuman agents who, capricious as their acts must often have appeared, were actuated by motives not wholly alien or wholly inscrutable. Hence they sought to propitiate these agents by honours and offerings, by sacrifices and worship—doing what they could to get the gods on their side.

This was early science: a Kuhnian paradigm, now out of fashion and unlikely to come in again;[7] not in itself unreasonable, although, in comparison with some later theories, poor in its yield of practical successes. Its importance in the present connection is obvious enough. For neither our knowledge of the causal efficacy of motive in general nor the theoretical extension of this model of causal efficacy to the sphere of the superhuman can with any plausibility be represented as resting on Humean foundations, that is on the observation of 'events repeatedly following in a uniform manner upon preceding appearances'. To say this is not of course to deny that we can learn about human motivation, or even fancy that we can learn about divine motivation, from experience. But, of this kind of learning, as of learning an enriched conception of the powers and propensities of non-animate things, it must be said that it presupposes an awareness, both general and specific, of causal propensity; and it should further be added that experience in this area normally works through a distinctive kind of advance in self-understanding or empathetic understanding, of which nothing resembling a Humean account can possibly be given.

VI

Theories of superhuman agency, never alone in the field, ultimately gave place, of course, to theories which, except in the field of human or animal action, made no reference to motives. The successor theories owed their succession to their greater success. The gains

---

[7] Perhaps we can find a lingering trace of it in the sense, on the part of some of the ecologically minded, that we have, as a species, been guilty in this century of impiety towards nature; for which we shall be made to pay.

from improved knowledge of causal propensity and causal power are not only improved understanding, but increased certainty of prediction and increased power of control. We have already seen how the notions of generality and normality of action and reaction are inseparable from those of causal propensity and power, themselves inseparable from the notions of types of substance or of natural kinds and of the qualities in respect of which individuals of the same kind may differ from each other; and it is easy to appreciate how practical and theoretical pressure alike will tend to drive enquiry in a certain direction: in the direction of an advance from mere regularities to invariabilities, from propensities to strict laws. For the demand for explanation is generated not only by ignorance of what characteristic circumstances induced a characteristic response or of what characteristic exercise of causal power produced a characteristic effect. It is generated also, and with greater poignancy, when the expected response or effect is not forthcoming, although the characteristic circumstances or exercise of power were observed to obtain or to occur; or, again, by the mere observation of differences in reaction to similar circumstances between things with similar general propensities.

These pressures arise then at the level of ordinary observation; and, as already remarked, we can go some way to refining our conceptions of the powers and propensities of things while remaining at that level. But we cannot go all the way to meet the theoretical pressure for strict law while remaining at that level. We can indeed say with confidence that when the brains are out, the man will die and there an end; or that a smart blow with a twenty-pound hammer will break an ordinary glass window. But such truths as these are insufficiently general to satisfy the theoretical pressure. To reach propositions which are sufficiently general and also have the character of strict law, we must abstract from the level of ordinary observation, abstract from all the complexity of circumstances characteristic of particular situations and confine ourselves to the terms of a particular physical theory. The procedure is reasonable, indeed necessary. But it does point to a great gap between our ordinary causal explanations of particular events and circumstances and the notion of explicit appeal to strict law.

This is a point on which Mill, for example, appears to have been thoroughly confused and to have confused his followers. Consider his account of the cause, 'philosophically speaking', as 'the sum total of the conditions, positive and negative, taken together; the whole of the contingencies of every description, which being realized, the consequent invariably follows'.[8] A man, say, falls down a flight of stone steps as he begins the descent. The steps are slippery and the man's mind is elsewhere. This is a sufficient explanation of his fall. But of course not every preoccupied man falls down every flight of slippery steps he descends. There is absolutely no question of our formulating or envisaging exceptionless laws, framed in terms of *this* order, to cover all such cases: no question of invoking 'contingencies' of various descriptions with the aim of achieving such a result. We do indeed suppose there to be exceptionless and truly general mechanical laws which bear on the case; but these are laws framed in terms of a quite different order, the relatively abstract terms of a physical theory. We have no prospect of knowing, and no interest in enquiring, in precise detail, just *how* these laws apply in such a particular case as that described. So Mill's account is quite curiously wide of the mark so far as ordinary causal explanation is concerned.

Having said so much, I may seem under some obligation to answer two questions about theoretical laws: how are such laws established? And how are they applied in practice, that is, how are they *used* to achieve desired effects? For such laws certainly are established, or come to be accepted as established; and they certainly are put to use—now as never before. These questions belong to the philosophy of science and of applied science; and anything like a generally adequate answer to them is beyond both my competence and the scope of this enquiry. But perhaps it is enough for present purposes to point out that the establishing of such laws requires, first, the framing of hypotheses and, second, that the hypotheses be tested, and perhaps given specific quantitative form, *in carefully contrived observational situations*, that is, situations so contrived that exact knowledge is possible of those features in the situation to which the putative law relates. (How such hypotheses themselves come to be

---

[8] *System of Logic*, III. v. 3.

framed I have earlier suggested in pointing to the role of models or analogies derived from ordinary observation of causal efficacy and to the progressive attenuation of their influence in the course of theoretical advance.) As for the practical application of such laws, this is again a matter of careful contrivance: of ensuring, as far as possible, that the conditions we produce answer to certain exact specifications *in respect of those features to which the law relates*. It is then a necessary truth that if we have succeeded in this, if the law in fact holds, and if we have done our calculations correctly, then the conditions we have produced will themselves produce, *as far as the relevant features are concerned*, the outcome we intend.

So much—and I know it is all too little—about the role of exceptionless law. Thinking, as we do, of the natural realm at a variety of different levels, or from a variety of theoretical and practical viewpoints, we may suppose that there is one level at which general, exceptionless, and discoverable law reigns throughout that realm. We are authoritatively told that there is another level—a lower or minuter level of physical theory—at which it does not; at which the most we can expect is probabilistic law. What I have been lately concerned to suggest is that the level of ordinary causal explanation of particular events and circumstances, the level at which we employ the common vocabulary of description rather than the technical vocabularies of physical theories, there is no reason to think that our explanations presuppose or rest upon belief in the existence of general, exceptionless, and discoverable laws frameable in terms of that common vocabulary; and that, further, there is no reason to think that our explanations are, for this reason, in any way deficient. I think I have, earlier on, said enough about the way in which the notion of causal action and reaction, of causal efficacy and propensity, is embodied in our common concepts to explain, if explanation is needed, how and why this is so.

VII

Before concluding, I wish to mention one odd philosophical consequence of adherence to the received view—or to an essential element in the received view—of causality; or, which is virtually the same thing, of neglect in the ways in which the notion of cause is actually embodied in our ordinary ideas of things. This essential element in the received view is the doctrine that, as far as its objective content is concerned, the notion of cause is reducible to that of invariability of association of types of occurrence or circumstance. The favoured terminology for handling this latter notion is the terminology of necessary and sufficient conditions. Thus we have such formulations as the following: if circumstances of a certain type, X, obtain, then the occurrence of an event of a certain type α is necessary and sufficient for the subsequent occurrence of an event of a certain type β. This scheme is clearly equivalent to: if circumstances of a certain type, X, obtain, then the occurrence of an event of a certain type β is sufficient and necessary for the prior occurrence of an event of a certain type α. Suppose circumstances of type X do obtain and particular events of types α and β do occur in that order. So far as necessity and sufficiency are concerned, we have no reason for calling the α-type event a, or the, cause of the β-type event rather than vice versa; no reason, indeed, for distinguishing between cause and effect at all rather than recognizing a symmetrical relation of, say, mutual causal dependence. Yet we seem to have an obstinate prejudice in favour of the view that there is such a distinction, and that, while causes may precede or be simultaneous with their effects, effects never precede their causes; and, further, that this is not to be understood as simply the consequence of a trivial verbal stipulation. So the received doctrine presents us with the problem of justifying, or at least explaining, our obstinate adherence to this view.

Once we turn our backs on the received doctrine, however, and consider together both the modes in which the notion of causality is embodied in our ordinary ideas and the association of this notion with that of explanation, we see that the supposed problem is quite spurious. Consider the two basic and connected models of (1) the exercise of mechanical power by a physical agent and (2) the motivation of a human agent; and note how the first model is present in the very naming of the second. Recall how the state of affairs which ensues upon the exercise of mechanical power—the pushing or the pulling—is explained by reference to that exercise; and how human action is explained by reference to the motives behind it. Recall again how any display of natural propensity is explained by the typical circumstances which excite it, to which it is a response or reaction. Here are natural asymmetries enough, and to spare, to show that the notion of priority which would, on the received view, appear as a trivial or whimsical addition to our concept of causal dependence, lies in fact at its very root. One might think it extraordinary that philosophers could manœuvre themselves into a position at which so fundamental a feature of so fundamental a concept should appear problematic; but perhaps, on second thoughts, one should recognize the fact as one of the glories of the subject.[9]

And now to conclude. If we take in our hand, as Hume would say, any volume, such as an old-fashioned novel or a book of traveller's reminiscences, which contains extended passages of narrative-cum-descriptive writing, we may not find in those passages many occurrences of the word 'cause'; but we shall find the pages stiff with verbs, transitive and intransitive, referring to a myriad modes of causal action and reaction. An account in such terms carries with it, in general, a sufficient explanation of the circumstances recorded—of why such-and-such a thing happened, of how such-and-such another came to pass. Sometimes, in such a text, causality will figure under its general name: for example, when the notion or question of

---

[9] Of course it is always open to ingenuity to describe imaginary situations in terms which encourage us to think of reversed causality as a possibility; but such descriptions generally owe their persuasive power to a perverse exploitation of concepts, such as those of observation or copying, which belong to our ordinary scheme. Evidently observation and copying involve causal dependence. Equally evidently it is impossible to copy or observe what has not yet come into existence. But the imaginary situations in question are described in terms which irresistibly put us in mind of these ordinary acts or relations while placing their pseudo-objects in what is, relative to them, the future. The essential feature of the trick is to describe isolated cases of the imagined kind, in order to play them off against the normal conceptual background. This is not to deny that it may be possible to describe imaginary cases which do not thus exploit ordinary causal concepts and yet similarly invite us to invert the ordinary temporal order of *explanation*. But so deep are the natural roots of the common concepts of *causal efficacy* and *causal dependence* that, even if we accepted the explanation, it is unclear that we should regard ourselves as employing, with inverted temporal application, those very concepts.

explanation or of mode of production of some particular circumstance is *explicitly* to the fore. And, of course, in a quite different kind of text, or of context, causality may figure under its general name in connection with the search for, or the discovery of, the *general* mechanism of production of some *general* type of effect; as when we speak of the cause of malaria or of cancer.

Should we then finally say—to end where we began—that 'cause' does name a relation which holds in nature between distinct existences? Or should we deny this and call it rather the name of a general categorial notion which we invoke in connection with the explanation of particular circumstances and the discovery of general mechanisms of production of general types of effect? I do not think it matters very much which we do. Indeed, the adoption of the second of these courses does not altogether exclude the first; for when we properly invoke one particular fact or conjunction of facts in explanation of another; and when the particular events and circumstances mentioned in the statement of the explaining and explained facts are indeed distinct existences; then, although the relation holds only because the particular events and circumstances are of the kinds described in the explaining and explained propositions, there seems no particular harm in saying that those particular events and circumstances, however described, do in fact stand in a particular relation which may be called causal.

❧ 10 ❧

Freedom and Necessity

FOR my final subject I turn to an issue which, in a variety of forms, has troubled and perplexed the reflective part of mankind for as long as any: the issue of the freedom, or lack of it, of the human will; and I choose, as the focus of discussion, two celebrated theses espoused by Spinoza in the *Ethics*.

According to the first of these theses, the sense of freedom of decision and action, which we experience daily, is nothing but illusion, since it implies a belief which is incompatible with the universal reign of natural causality. According to the second thesis, this illusory sense of freedom is itself caused by a combination of two factors: on the one hand, our *consciousness* of our actions, decisions, and desires and, on the other hand, our *ignorance* of their causes. Both theses are open to question. I shall give reasons for questioning, indeed for rejecting, both of them.

That we have a sense of freedom, that we necessarily act, as Kant says, under the *idea* of freedom, is generally allowed. That this sense entails a belief incompatible with the universal reign of natural causality is frequently denied; by Kant for dubiously intelligible reasons; by others for more pedestrian reasons. The pedestrian compatibilist will maintain, not that free actions are free from all causality, but that they are free from certain kinds of causality—the causality, he will say, of constraint; and he will be ready enough to illustrate what he means by this with examples of physical force or intrusive psychological compulsion.

One who, on this ground, questions the first thesis is under an obligation of consistency to question also the second—the thesis about the causal source of the sense of freedom. He can scarcely allow that knowledge of causes would make those causes constraining which were not so before; and he would surely be hardly more willing to allow that such knowledge would cause an authentic sense of freedom to be replaced by an illusion of constraint. So, it seems, he must deny that the sense of freedom is caused by ignorance of causes. And then, in all intellectual decency, he may feel obliged to give another account of the source of that sense.

Can these requirements be met? At one level at least, they can. Men are not generally ignorant of the immediate causes of their actions: they often enough know what combinations of desire, preference, belief, and perception prompt them to act as they do. Not all their reasons are rationalizations. As for the remoter causes of their actions, i.e. the causes of their own desires, dispositions, and preferences, they will often enough have a reasonably accurate notion of the sources of these as well, acknowledging both the general determining power of education, training, environment, and heredity and the specific influence of this or that element of these determining forces. Blank ignorance of causes does not exist; so the sense of freedom cannot be attributed to such ignorance. Whence, then, does this sense arise? Or, better perhaps, what does it consist in?

Here one can only sketch an answer. First, we should consider that our desires and preferences are not, in general, something we just note in ourselves as alien presences. To a large extent they *are* we. The point gains force from the very fact of exceptions to it: i.e. from the presence in some subjects, sometimes, of dispositions and desires which they do experience as intrusive compulsions. In respect of them, there is no sense of freedom, but its absence is not attributable to knowledge of their causes; on the contrary, the sufferers from such compulsions may suffer also from just such ignorance of their causes as Spinoza would declare to be the source of the sense of freedom.

Second, we should consider the experience of deliberation and relate this experience to the point that our desires and preferences are not, in general, something we just note in ourselves as alien presences. A corollary of this point is that, in the experience of deliberation, we are not mere spectators of a scene in which—setting aside the element of reckoning, of calculation—contending desires struggle for mastery with ourselves as prize. This image may sometimes be appropriate, but it is not the image appropriate to the standard experience of deliberation. That experience heightens our sense of self; in the higher-order desire which determines what we call our choice we identify ourselves the more completely; and this is why we call it our choice.

Finally, we should consider the experience of agency. When a basic action of ours issues by a normal causal route from a specific intention of so acting, which itself issues from a combination of relevant belief and desire, then we have immediate knowledge, not only that our action has been such as we intended to perform, but also that it has been performed intentionally. As has been pointed out by recent writers in the theory of action, it can sometimes happen that someone acts as he intended to act yet does not perform that action intentionally. The action may issue causally from the appropriate combination of desire and belief, but the causal route from desire and belief to action may be of the wrong kind. The anticipatory thought of action may, for example, so disturb or unnerve us that we find ourselves *unintentionally* making just such a bodily movement as we *intended* to make—as letting go the rope which holds up the fellow mountaineer, in a famous example of Professor Davidson's. In such cases the experience of agency is lacking. The cases are worth mentioning in order to emphasize the fact that the experience is normally present, and to remind us of what it is like.

Here, then, is a part at least of the phenomenology of the sense of freedom. The fact that we find ourselves in our desires and preferences and do not, in general, find them as alien presences within ourselves; the experience of deliberation which heightens and strengthens our sense of self; and the constantly repeated experience of agency—all these contribute to, perhaps constitute, the sense of freedom. Experiencing it ourselves, we attribute it also to others.

Suppose it is acknowledged that the sense of freedom, so regarded, experienced in ourselves and attributed to others, is a natural fact; not, in general, causally threatened by knowledge of

particular causes, nor logically threatened by a general belief in the
reign of universal causality; not logically threatened because not a
belief and hence not a belief incompatible with that general belief.
Yet the sense of freedom, this natural fact, is closely linked with
other attitudes to ourselves and others, with other feelings towards
ourselves and others and with other concepts which we apply to
ourselves and others; and it is often argued that the justification of
some of these attitudes and feelings and of the application of some of
these concepts requires, and is seen by us to require, the truth
of beliefs which *are* incompatible with the general belief in the
universal reign of natural causality. Spinoza speaks of the notions of
sin and merit, praise and blame, and of allied emotions. In general,
we may say, what are at issue are the notions, attitudes, and feelings
associated with moral judgement, with the idea of moral desert. Now
it certainly is generally held—it is a thesis, one might say, of the
common moral consciousness—that the appropriateness of these
attitudes and feelings, the applicability of these notions, requires, in
respect of any occasion on which these attitudes and notions are in
question, that the agent *could have acted otherwise* than he did on that
occasion. But—so the argument runs—if the thesis of determinism
is true, then it is not true of any agent on any occasion that that agent
could have acted otherwise than he did on that occasion. Hence, if
the thesis of determinism is true, the attitudes and notions in
question are never appropriate.

Is the thesis of the common moral consciousness correctly
interpreted in this line of reasoning? Is it really the case that our
belief in the appropriateness of the attitudes and feelings in question,
or in the just applicability of the relevant notions—is it really the
case that this belief depends in its turn on other beliefs which are
incompatible with the determinist thesis?

It is certainly true that often, in the context of a moral judgement
(especially if disapprobative) one may utter the words, 'He could
have acted otherwise', or other words to the same effect. But are
such words, as then uttered, really equivalent to 'There was no
sufficient natural impediment or bar, *of any kind whatsoever, however
complex*, to his acting otherwise'? I find it difficult, as others have
found it difficult, to accept this equivalence. The common judge-

ment of this form amounts rather to the denial of any sufficient natural impediment *of certain specific kinds or ranges of kinds.* For example, 'He could (easily) have helped them (instead of withholding help)' may amount to the denial of any lack on his part of adequate muscular power or financial means. Will the response, 'It simply wasn't in his nature to do so' lead to a withdrawal of moral judgement in such a case? I hardly think so; rather to its reinforcement.

There is another reason, equally familiar, for questioning the proposed equivalence. Acceptance of the equivalence commits one to the view that the practice of moral appraisal is either rationally grounded on, or causally dependent on, the conscious or tacit rejection of the thesis of determinism. But when those who accept the equivalence are invited to enlarge on the question, how a belief in the absence of determining causes explains or justifies the practices and attitudes in question, their answers are singularly insufficient. It is hard to see how randomness, or a belief in randomness, could either explain or justify any such thing; and attempts to formulate the belief in other terms have never resulted in anything but either high-flown nonsense or psychological descriptions which are in no way incompatible with the thesis of determinism. No one has ever been able to state intelligibly what that state of affairs, that condition of freedom, which has been supposed to be necessary to ground our moral attitudes and judgements, would actually consist in. The question, 'If we believe in such a condition, what exactly are we believing?', remains unanswered and, I think, unanswerable.

Some who have faced this fact, but have also felt, or thought they felt, an irreconcilable tension between the reign of causality and the holding of moral attitudes, have concluded that there is something inherently confused about moral attitudes. This conclusion echoes Spinoza.

Nevertheless it is the wrong conclusion to draw; or, at least, drawn in this way and for this reason, it is wrongly drawn. Our proneness to moral attitudes and feelings is a natural fact, just as the sense of freedom is a natural fact. I have remarked that they are linked, and it is time to say more about the link. In speaking of the sense of freedom, I connected it closely with the sense of self. Our desires, decisions, actions are not in general felt as alien, as things that simply happen in or to us, like a pain or a blow. They are we. Our awareness of them is awareness of ourselves. I remarked that we attribute to others this same sense of freedom and this same sense of self. We see others as other selves, and are aware that they so see each other. But this is not a matter of a conclusion drawn by analogical reasoning. In a variety of ways, inextricably bound up with the facts of mutual human involvement and interaction, we *feel* towards each other as to other selves; and this variety is just the variety of moral and personal reactive attitudes and emotions which we experience towards others and which have their correlates in attitudes and emotions directed towards ourselves.[1] Of all, or most, of these emotions and attitudes, whether self-directed or other-directed, Spinoza himself treats in the *Ethics*. He treats of them as natural facts, bringing unparalleled psychological insight to bear on the detailed analysis of their causes and effects. For this analysis one can have nothing but admiration. What I have been concerned to dispute is the thesis that these emotions and attitudes, together with the associated sense of freedom, of self and of other selves, rest upon a belief, or beliefs, incompatible with the doctrine of the universal reign of natural causality.

But we must again distinguish. There is the thesis that these emotions and attitudes, together with the sense of freedom, rest upon *false belief*. And there is the thesis that this cluster of associated feelings rests upon *ignorance*: upon ignorance of the actual causes of desires, dispositions, and actions. Clearly the two theses are logically independent. The second could be true even if the first were false. Earlier I summarily rejected the second thesis, as far as the sense of freedom was concerned, as well as the first. At least I rejected it in its full generality, arguing that we could have a reasonably accurate notion of the causal sources of our desires and dispositions and those of others—as well as of our actions and theirs—without being in the least disposed, as a result of this knowledge, to lose our sense of these desires, dispositions, and actions as truly ours (or theirs), to lose our sense of our (or their) selves and our (or their) freedom in

---

[1] I have written at greater length of these attitudes in 'Freedom and Resentment', *Proceedings of the British Academy* (1962), reprinted variously.

respect of them; whereas, on the other hand, we could sometimes experience as alien compulsions, in respect of which we had no sense of freedom, certain desires and dispositions of the cause of which we were truly ignorant, which we were quite at a loss to account for.

Yet further consideration of the second thesis is called for. I have spoken of a kind of non-specialist knowledge which we have of the sources of human dispositions, desires, and actions. We explain ourselves and others to ourselves and others in terms which we might call human and social terms. We refer to inherited traits, to social influences, to the effects of education, training, and experience, to the particular circumstances in which people find themselves. We speak of character and personality and the influences which form and modify them. We can develop considerable subtlety and expertise in this kind of knowledge. But it remains a relatively vague and inexact kind of knowledge; and there must be few who suppose that it will ever be anything else.

But we are also, and increasingly, able to view ourselves in a quite different kind of light—that of the physical and biological sciences; to see ourselves, in that light, as genetically programmed mechanisms of immense complexity, mechanisms constantly modified by their own history and responding, in constantly modified ways, to sensory inputs with behavioural outputs. The scope for the development of these sciences is no less immense than the complexity of the mechanisms which we must take ourselves to be; and we are only at the threshold of this development. Nevertheless the knowledge which these sciences deliver and promise differs in a fundamental respect from that knowledge of the causation of human behaviour which I have just spoken of; for it is, as far as it goes, *exact* knowledge. Let us suppose, then, that we were able to give complete causal explanations of human behaviour, including our own, in terms belonging to these exact sciences. Suppose, in a spirit entirely Spinozistic, that we were able to identify every thought, feeling, original impulse to action, with—or as the 'mental' aspect or correlate of—some complex physical state of which we could, in turn, determine the sufficient physical causes, tracing the latter as far back as we needed or wished to. Might we not then be said to have replaced our present, inexact, inadequate knowledge and understanding of the causes of our desires, dispositions, and actions with adequate knowledge and understanding? And might not such adequate knowledge remove the basis of the sense of freedom and the sense of self and hence of the associated moral and personal attitudes and emotions—thus vindicating the thesis that these last did indeed rest, if not on absolute ignorance, then at least on inadequate knowledge, of causes?

The suggestion involves obvious minor complications, inasmuch as such mental items as the sense of agency, say, or the sense of guilt, must themselves be supposed to have physical correlates and physical causes; so it would at least be necessary to suppose substantial modifications in the mechanism itself to result from knowledge of its workings. But it is pointless to dwell on these complications; for the question which contains the suggestion is unanswerable. It is unanswerable because the supposition which gives rise to it could not conceivably be fulfilled. X, let us say, notices that Y's last remark has caused embarrassment to Z and, wishing to spare Z's feelings, X himself makes a remark intended to change the direction of the conversation. Can we seriously con-template the possibility of being able to give, in terms belonging exclusively to the exact physical sciences, a complete causal account of the origin of precisely this complex of thought, feeling, and action on X's part? And of every other piece of human behaviour of even such modest complexity as this? The idea is absurd; and not because there would not be world enough and time to work out the solutions to such particular problems, as there is not world enough and time to work out the particular causal conditions of every movement of a leaf on the surface of a stream. It is more fundamentally absurd because there is no practical possibility of establishing the general principles on which any such calculation would have to be based. This does not mean that we must absolutely deny the existence of underlying psycho-physical correlations even in such cases as these. It does not mean that the idea of such correlations, in such cases, must remain merely an idea—something quite without effect, quite empty in a practical point of view. So for the explanation of X's behaviour, we must have recourse to the inexactitudes of: 'That is the sort of man he is—and he has a tenderness for Z—and he is that sort of man partly because he was brought up in *that* society—and Z appeals to him because . . .'; and so on.

There is, of course, more to be said about the scope of physical explanations of human behaviour. First, if the fine connections, envisaged above, between the language of the exact sciences on the one hand and the language of mind and behaviour on the other are unattainable, grosser connections *are* attainable. Many general kinds of dependence of the mental and behavioural on the physical are well enough known. We can modify perception, stimulate memory, reduce or enhance aggression, depression, or sexual drive, say, by chemical or electrical means. A great extension of this kind of knowledge is to be foreseen; and knowledge of such dependences, and of the availability of techniques for exploiting them, may surely, in certain cases, contribute to inhibiting those personal and moral attitudes and reactions whose basis is at issue, or at least to lessening their force. So why, it may be asked, should this inhibiting effect not be generalized? All the general traits which manifest themselves in particular episodes of human behaviour, however *nuancé* may be the descriptions we are inclined to give of those episodes, must, we suppose, have a physical base. So why should the inhibiting effect of such knowledge be confined to certain cases? I think the answer (or the beginnings of the answer) is to be found in first noting the fact that these are also the cases which we are favourably disposed to regarding as 'cases for treatment'. They are the cases in which the traits in question are displayed in a form which, of itself, tends to inhibit ordinary interpersonal attitudes in favour of 'objective' attitudes. Another part of the answer consists in the obvious point that the general, and surely justified, belief in the physical basis of mind is something very different from, and falls far short of, such detailed and particular knowledge of psycho-physical correspondences as I earlier declared to be out of the question. It is for these two reasons, then, that our knowledge of general kinds of dependence of the mental on the physical can be said only to contribute, and only in certain cases, to modifying or inhibiting personal and moral reactions and attitudes. But the matter is complicated, and doubtless deserves fuller treatment than I accord it here.

The second point to be made about the scope of physical

explanations of human behaviour is this. I gave above a particular example of such behaviour and described it in the ordinary human terms of intention and motive. I dismissed the idea of being able, even in principle, to give adequate causal explanations of such episodes, *so described*, in the terms of the exact sciences. But suppose we were content to abandon the practice of describing behaviour in terms of intentional action in favour of describing it solely in terms of bodily movements. The general principles of exact and adequate causal explanation of behaviour, so understood, would no longer seem beyond our grasp; for the mechanisms of bodily movement show no discontinuity with the finer electro-chemical mechanisms of the human frame. The difficulties of explanation in particular cases would not be different in kind, though doubtless different in degree, from those of explaining the movements of the leaf on the stream.

I make this point only for the sake of completeness. What we were to contest was the thesis that knowledge of the causes of behaviour would undermine a certain range of attitudes and feelings. I pointed out that such general knowledge of causes as we actually possess has not in fact produced this effect. To the hypothetical question whether exact or 'adequate' knowledge would not produce it I respond with a distinction. So long as what we understand by 'human behaviour' is intentional action, such knowledge is unattainable. If we were to exclude from the description of human behaviour all reference to belief, desire, and intention, if we were to see it as consisting simply in bodily movement, then such knowledge might indeed be in principle attainable. But this truth is simply irrelevant to the issue before us. To see human behaviour as consisting simply of physical movement would, *of itself*, exclude the attitudes and feelings in question; for it is only in relation to behaviour understood, or experienced, as intentional action that these attitudes and feelings ever arise.

Index